Fiendish Ingenuity

An illustrated look at

Torture Throughout The Ages

Contents

	PAGE
Introduction	8
Breaking On The Wheel	11
Skinning Alive	14
Tortured On A Globe	17
Removal Of The Tongue	19
Broken In A Mortar	22
Roasting and Pricking	24
Frying Alive and Castration	27
Whipped and Nipples and Breasts Pulled Off	30
Sewn In Animal Skins and Thrown To The Dogs	32
Crucifixion	35
Burned At The Stake	38
Impaling	41
Thrown To Wild Beasts	44
Boiling To Death	47
Flagellation	49
Thrown From Cliffs	52

Hanging And Gibbeting	54
Decapitation	60
Broiled Alive	63
Peine forte et dure	66
Stoning	69
Suspended By One Arm	72
Clubbed To Death	75
Sharp Implements Forced Underneath Fingernails	78
Executed By Saw	81
Tearing Of Skin	84
Insect Torture	87
Dragged Along The Ground	91
Suffocation	95
Suffocation By Drowning	100
Forced Ingestion Of A Liquid	106
Disembowelment	109
The Disembowelment of Pregnant Women	113
Removal Of Heart	117
The Rack	121

Children Butchered	125
Displaying Dismembered Body Parts	130
Torture Of The Boots	134
Forced To Carry Weight	139
Twisted Cords Torture and Execution	144
The Burning of Multiple Victims	149
Tortured by Using Animals	154
Cords Through Limbs	159
Drawing and Quartering	162
Conclusion	163

List of Illustrations

	PAGE
Broken On The Wheel	10
Skinning Alive	13
Tortured On A Globe	16
Ripping Out Of Tongue	18
Broken In A Mortar	21
Roasting and Pricking	23
Frying Alive and Castration	26
Whipped and Nipples Pulled Off	29
Sewn In Animal Skins and Thrown To The Dogs	31
Crucifixion	34
Burned At The Stake	37
Impaling	40
Thrown To Wild Beasts	43
Boiling To Death	46
Flagellation	48
Thrown From Cliffs	51
Hung Upon A Gibbet	53

Hung By The Legs Until Dead	56
Decapitation	59
Broiled Alive	62
Peine forte et dure	65
Stoning	68
Suspended By One Arm	71
Clubbed To Death	74
Sharp Implements Forced Underneath Fingernails	77
Executed By Saw	80
Tearing Of Skin	83
Insect Torture	86
Dragged Along The Ground	90
Suffocation	94
Christians suffocated with smoke	97
Suffocation By Drowning	99
Forced Ingestion Of A Liquid	105
Disembowelment	108
The Disembowelment of Pregnant Women	112
Removal Of Heart	116
The Rack	120

Children Butchered	124
Displaying Dismembered Body Parts	129
Torture Of The Boots	133
Forced To Carry Weight	138
Twisted Cords Torture and Execution	143
The Burning of Multiple Victims	148
Tortured by Using Animals	153
Animals and Dungeons	156
Cords Through Limbs	158
Drawing and Quartering	161

INTRODUCTION

The propensity for man to torture his fellow man is as old as civilisation itself and, although in modern times sometimes taking on more sophisticated guises, it shows very little sign of diminishing. It has always been the universal practice for society and the state to attempt to justify torture by placing it in the category of punishment, thereby denying its use. There is of course, *no* rigid line between torture and the concept of punishment; it is largely dependent upon the perception of the individual victim concerned and their physical and mental reaction to the suffering experienced, as to whether something can be described as torture or not. In the case of psychological torture, a form of punishment considered relatively mild by one individual, might constitute a most horrible form of torture to another.

However, it would be a mistake to classify every form of punishment, in all circumstances, as torture. The majority of punishments inflicted in civilized countries under state law certainly *do not* fall into the category of physical torture. Even in places in the world where capital punishment still exists, as odious as it may be, death deliberately induced by the state does not in itself rank as a form of *physical torture* (although the psychological aspects of such an execution may be quite another matter).

Physical torture by its very nature, whether or not it precedes death implies unjustifiable suffering or pain, and it is within this paradigm that the present work exists. The illustrations contained within theses pages are taken from Samuel Clarke's "A Generall Martyrologie" London 1651. I have chosen these plates because, although somewhat naive in execution, they accurately portray many of the categories of torture that have been practised throughout the ages and are, I feel, as forceful to the eye as the terrible tortures that they describe.

I would advise the reader that the verbal descriptions supplied by Clarke (with spelling as in the original text), that I have used to explain the illustrations, need to be read a little tongue in cheek. Clarke was a passionate Protestant and regarded the Catholic religion as an anathema to Christianity. His descriptions, therefore, appear to be a little fanciful and tend to over emphasize the cruelty of the Catholics and the godliness of the Protestants. There is no doubt that the Catholics did torture the Protestants, but equally, there is no doubt that the Protestants tortured the Catholics when the opportunity arose. There is also no doubt that *both* parties tortured every other poor, unfortunate creature that did not happen to agree with their spiritual philosophies.

The often well thought out, although invariably diabolical methods, that human beings have devised, not only to inflict pain and suffering on one another, but on the animal kingdom as a whole, are as widespread today as they always were. The following pages concentrate solely on this one aspect of mans' nature; his fiendish ingenuity when it comes to devising methods of inflicting pain and suffering on others.

The historical accuracy with regard to every single name, date, and event, mentioned in this work I cannot guarantee; to check every historical source used would be an exhaustive if not a futile task. Although intended to be as accurate as possible, the main aim of the book, and what I can guarantee, is that the tortures and torturous implements herein described, were *most definitely* used at some point during our violent and bloody past.

PLATE 1.

Broken On The Wheel

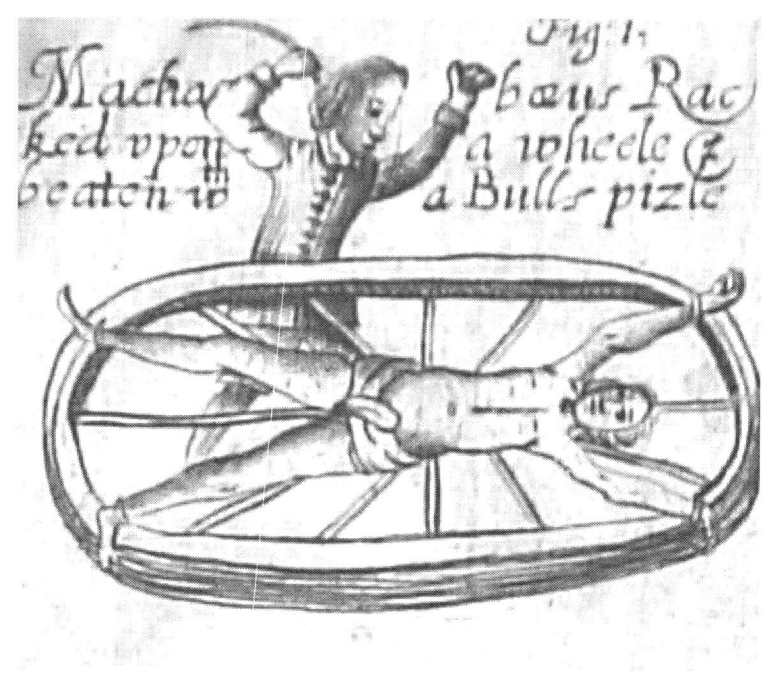

Breaking On The Wheel

This method of execution, a most ancient one, involved prolonged agony before the occurrence of death and possibly at one time held a religious significance. It is a method that came in various forms; from binding the victim upon a broad wheel resembling a cylinder and rolling it down a hill or mountain, often over iron spikes fixed in the ground, to a method where heavy wagons were driven over the victim's body again and again until all their bones were broken. The most common form of breaking on the wheel practised in Europe between the sixteenth and eighteenth century was similar to the one pictured, (see PLATE 1). The victim was spread-eagled and tied face uppermost onto a large cartwheel which often had the ability to be rotated so that the executioner could bring the victim's targeted limb to within easy reach of his weapon. Often in place of a cart wheel a couple of wooden beams in the shape of a St. Andrew's cross would suffice. Whatever the shape of the device the misery the victim would endure would always be the same.

The executioner armed with an iron bar, long handled hammer or heavy club, methodically smashed to pieces the limbs of his victim before finally putting him (although there are reported cases of women being executed in this way) out of his misery with a blow to the stomach, heart, or neck.

It must also be remembered that these types of executions were generally carried out in public. In order for the crowd to enjoy the grisly spectacle a little more, the wheel was sometimes slightly canted to give them a better view. However, giving the crowd a better view was one thing, but there are recorded instances where the crowd actually participated in the brutal proceedings. In St. Domingo on the 28

September, 1791, at the time of a rebellion there, two prisoners were broken on two pieces of timber placed crosswise. The first prisoner after having each arm and leg broken was mercifully finished off with a killer blow to the stomach. The second prisoner was not so fortunate. After breaking the prisoner's arms and legs, the executioner was about to deliver the killer blow when a mob of spectators forced him to stop. They then took the prisoner, who by this time was writhing in agony, to a cart-wheel and securely tied him to it. Hoisting the cart-wheel into the air and fixing the other end of the wheel axel into the ground they left the cart wheel with its broken cargo suspended in the air while they gloated over the terrible agonies the prisoner was suffering. The poor prisoner endured this agony for a full forty minutes before some English seaman who had witnessed this barbarous act, finished the prisoner off, by strangling him.

The picture referred to earlier (see PLATE 1), is Samuel Clarke's representation of Maccabeus the eldest of seven brothers, who along with their mother Salamona, were brought before the tyrant Antiochus. After the family were beaten with bulls-pizzles (bull's penises), Maccabeus was singled out for further torment. Not only was he to endure the torture of the wheel but he was first stripped, stretched out upon the rack and viciously beaten. He was then placed upon the wheel where heavy weights were suspended from his feet in order to break his body. No killer blow for poor Maccabeus. A fire was lit and he was thrown into it; the flames burning him so badly that his bowels became exposed. Still alive, he was taken from the fire, his tongue pulled out, and then finally, he was fried to death.

PLATE 2.

𝒮𝓀𝒾𝓃𝓃𝒾𝓃𝑔 𝒜𝓁𝒾𝓋𝑒

Skinning Alive

Skinning alive or flaying is an old method of torture used to condemn the victim to a long lingering death and was popular in China and other eastern countries; in Turkey it was much used for the crime of piracy. It is also said to have been the chosen method of torture by Asdrubal, who lived in the second century before Christ, and was the founder of the new Carthage.

Although not so popular in Europe, flaying was not unknown. In 1366, the Chamberlain of the Count de Rucci was executed in this way and in 1655, four years after the illustrations I am using were first published, Jacopo Perrin and his brother, David, had their arms and legs flayed during the persecutions of the religious sect known as the Waldenses.

Akin to flaying, is the technique of scalping adopted by the North American Indians. The method they employed was to grasp the hair on the crown of the head of their victim (usually with their left hand), bring the knife around it and slice into the skin, tearing off the skin with the hair. This resulted in them removing a piece of skin and hair approximately 4 inches in diameter. Owing to this rough and ready practice most of the victims died but there were a few exceptions.

The practice of scalping was not restricted purely to the Indians. Herodotus (c.484 BC - c.425 BC), refers to scalping being practised by the Scythians when he says they killed their enemies by cutting a circle around their captive's neck just below the ears and stripping off their skin.

In the pioneer days of America, when the white settlers were prone to call the Indians savages, they too, were not averse to taking a few Indian scalps, although in their case their motives were a little different from the Indians. Whereas the Indians believed the scalps that they took held magical powers, i.e. the powers of their previous owners, the whites hunted scalps purely for monetary reasons. Not to be outdone; the British offered bounties for French scalps and the French returned the favour by offering bounties for British scalps. Being told to "keep your hair on!" in those days seems to have been pretty sound advice.

For a more comprehensive example of flaying, turn to Samuel Clarke's picture of Aber being skinned alive (see PLATE 2). Aber, the second eldest of the brothers of that ill fated family, was the next victim of the pitiless Antiochus. His hands were bound with iron chains and in this way he was suspended in the air. His skin was then stripped from the crown of his head to his knees allowing his entrails to become exposed. As if this was not enough, it is said that in this bloody and agonised state he was thrown to a leopard, which for some reason, refused to eat him.

PLATE 3.

Tortured On A Globe

Tortured On A Globe

This is the only example (see PLATE 3.) of this type of torture that I have come across in my research. It does; however, appear to be yet another version of 'breaking on the wheel'. I would have thought that the idea would have been to roll the victim over the ground to cause injury but according to Samuel Clark who obtained his information from 'Josephus and the Books of the Maccabees', this was not the case. He says that Antiochus caused Machir (the third eldest of the boys) "to be tied about it in such sort that all his bones were put out of joint, hanging one from another in a most pitiful manner."

Like his brothers before him, this was not the only torture Machir was to suffer. While still mounted on the globe the skin of his head and face was pulled off. He was then placed upon the wheel, but little more damage could be done, as all of his bones were already dislocated and his face and body were bleeding profusely. His tongue was cut out and as a final humiliation he was fried to death in a large frying pan.

PLATE 4.

Removal Of The Tongue

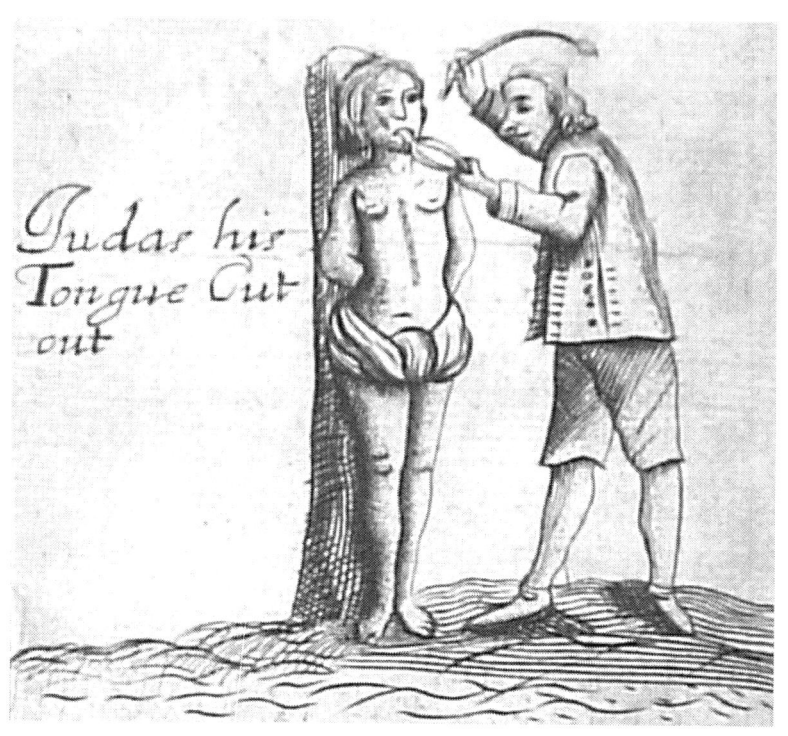

Removal Of The Tongue

In France, the removal of the tongue was a popular method of torture for blasphemy although it was also used for other offences. According to Frederic Shoberl in 'Persecutions of Popery'; in Abbeville in 1766, a young officer, the Chevalier de la Barre, was accused of mutilating the figure on a wooden crucifix which stood on the bridge of Abbeville. With very little evidence to support this charge, other than the accused was accustomed to singing bawdy songs and that he had read the heretical works of Voltaire, he was sentenced to be put to torture and have his tongue cut out. He was seventeen years old.

One account involving tongue removal is recorded in 'Pitcairn's Trials' and is as brutal as anyone could wish to read. In this particular case the victim was mercifully dead when his tongue was removed but his suffering beforehand must have been unbearable. In 1623, members of the clan McFarlane were charged with and convicted for the murder of George Buchanan. The McFarlanes and the Buchanans were two feuding clans and at about eight o'clock one morning, several members of the McFarlane clan came across George Buchanan walking his four dogs. They seized him and bound him to a tree trunk and up until ten o'clock that night they tortured him each hour by administering three cuts with a dirk to parts of his body that would bring as much distress as possible but without killing him.

When they did finally kill the poor man, they stripped him of his clothing, cut his throat, and then cut out his tongue. The four dogs fared no better; the McFarlanes killed them, cutting one of the dog's tongue out and placing it in Buchanan's mouth whilst placing *his* tongue in the dog's mouth. Not content with that they removed the entrails of another dog and after slitting open the naked body of the murdered man removed his entrails and replaced them with the dog's. They then put Buchanan's entrails into the butchered dog and left the grisly scene for all to see.

Another instance of serial torture is illustrated on PLATE 4. Here, Judas, the fourth brother of the ill fated family, after being bound to a stake, was beaten and had his tongue ripped out. After suffering further mutilation he ended his life on the wheel.

PLATE 5.

𝓑roken 𝓘n 𝓐 𝓜ortar

Broken In A Mortar

An uncommon method of torture (see PLATE 5.) which shows Achas, the fifth brother of the family, placed into a brazen pot and his head pressed down towards his feet. The torture that he underwent appears to have combined forcing him down into a very confined space to make him as uncomfortable as possible and then beating down upon his head and upper body with a heavy implement. Regardless of how painful that must have been for Achas, he still afterwards, had to endure many of the other tortures his brothers had been subjected to.

The only other example of this mode of torture I have come across was reported in the 'Spectator' (23 December, 1893). The correspondent claims that "under the old Burmese regime, on the 'testimony of an eye witness,' the children of traitors were pounded with heavy pestles in wooden mortars."

PLATE 6.

Roasting and Pricking

Roasting and Pricking

The sixth brother to undergo the diabolical tortures ordered by the tyrant Antiochus (see PLATE 6.), was Areth. He was tied to a pillar head downwards and a fire was lit at such a distance away from him, so as not to fatally burn him, but to slowly roast him. He was further tortured by being pricked all over his head, face and body with awls to allow the heat to penetrate deeper into his skin. During these torments a great deal of blood and froth gathered about his face and head and as if that wasn't enough, he had his tongue pulled out with red hot pincers. Finally, like Maccabeus and Machir, he was destined to end his life in the frying pan.

The pricking torture that Areth endured is reminiscent of the pricking torture, under the guise of a test for the devil's mark that witches underwent during the days of witch-hunting. It was generally recognized that a witch would carry the mark of Satan and that the mark could be of two types: visible or invisible. The visible marks were easily discoverable, being birth marks, extra teats, moles, warts or any spot of unusual appearance. But how did the interrogators find the invisible mark? The witch-finders of the time were nothing if not ingenious: They came to the conclusion that if any part of the skin was insensitive to pain or did not bleed when punctured by the sharpest of implements, it must be an invisible badge of the devil. King James I, in his treatise on witchcraft, said that the absence of blood while 'pricking' was an infallible sign of sorcery.

Whenever a woman was accused of witchcraft, and believe me there were many, the revolting procedure of the 'bleeding test' was carried out. The woman would be stripped naked, have her hair shaved off and a witch-finder, who was usually paid by results, would slowly begin to torture her. Taking a long thin needle, he would systematically pierce all of the poor woman's body until he could discover a spot that failed to yield blood or the accused woman no longer cried out in pain. The test was invariably successful because either as a result of the continuous torture the woman's body would have become insensitive to pain through shock, or because the woman, to avoid going through further torture, would cease to give any indication of pain. There is of course, a third more sinister explanation for the success of this most damning test.

Mathew Hopkins, who excelled in the discovery of witches by 'pricking', operated throughout the eastern part of England between the years 1644 and 1647. This cunning sadist was responsible for the death of over two hundred women who, unknowingly, really did have the cards stacked up against them. He possessed a trick needle that telescoped into the handle, giving the impression that it had penetrated the woman's flesh without causing pain or drawing blood. If all else failed to confirm the woman's guilt, Hopkins could always rely on this trick.

PLATE 7.

Frying Alive and Castration

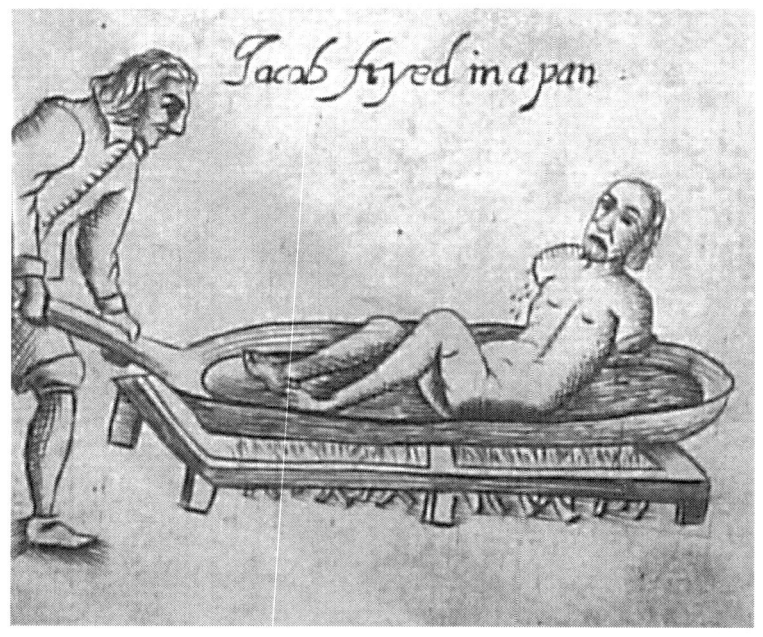

Frying Alive and Castration

To be fried alive was the final fate of most of the ill fated Maccabee family. A very old form of execution, the procedure consisted of placing the victim in a large shallow receptacle or dish, containing oil, tallow or pitch and then frying them alive. A variation on this theme was to place the victim on a gridiron or metal platform and light a fire underneath, thereby broiling the victim to death.

PLATE 7., shows Jacob, the youngest of the seven brothers, being fried alive. Before this extremely painful death, Jacob was also extensively tortured like his brothers before him. Bleeding profusely from his nose mouth and privy parts, Jacob had his hands and arms cut off and his tongue pulled out. The fact that Jacob was bleeding profusely from his privy parts suggests that he may well have been castrated.

Of all the terrible mutilations inflicted on people, whether for penal, religious, or purely vengeful reasons, castration has been one of the most frequently used. The torture associated with castration is of two kinds:

Firstly, there is of course the intense agony and great danger to life; the operation very often being carried out in a crude manner. Secondly, there is the psychological torture of any man who is castrated or even *threatened* with castration against his will, (as I'm sure any male reader will fully appreciate). It was this dread of castration that enabled the Egyptian Alexander to say that the deterrent effect of such a punishment was sufficient to prevent rape. Unfortunately, Alexander was only referring to the rape of *free* women, presumably the punishment did not extend to the rape of female slaves.

Over the centuries, in civilized countries,

castration as a judicial form of punishment has declined. However, it has been employed by mobs taking the law into their own hands and by individuals seeking private vengeance especially in relation to sexual crimes.

PLATE 8.

Whipped and Nipples Pulled Off

Whipped and Nipples and Breasts Pulled Off

Salamona, having gone through the torment of watching her seven sons cruelly tortured to death, was now stripped and hung up by the hands (see PLATE 8.). She was cruelly whipped and her nipples and breasts were pulled off, before she too, was consigned to the frying pan.

The mutilation of women's breasts, as obnoxious as it may seem, was carried out by the Turks on entering Austria in the sixteenth century and, closer to home, by Irish Catholics to Protestant women in the seventeenth century. During the persecutions of the Waldenses, in the valleys of Piedmont, a young woman called Martha Constantine was raped and then killed by having her breasts cut off. More recent examples of this barbarous act can still be found (see page 111 for more recent cases).

PLATE 9.

Sewn In Animal Skins and Thrown To The Dogs

Sewn In Animal Skins and Thrown To The Dogs

The Roman emperors were justifiably noted for their cruelty and barbarity to any poor soul that was unfortunate enough to incur their wrath. The sewing up of prisoners in wolves' skins so that they could be torn to bits by savage dogs was a particular favourite of the emperor Nero. The tyrant Nero pursued a course of unexampled debauchery and cruelty for a period of nearly fourteen years and it is to his barbarous reign that Samuel Clarke's illustration (see PLATE 9.) directly refers.

Maximinus, who lived and died a tyrant, was another Roman emperor that would sew up his victims in the skins of slaughtered animals, but in his case he would just leave the poor wretches to die slowly of starvation.

The involvement of dogs in mans' cruelties is, of course, not just restricted to Nero. One particularly nasty occurrence of their use is recorded in the savage wave of terror that took place in Ireland in 1642, when the Irish Papists attacked the English Protestants. In Kilkenny (see page 110), they hung up Protestant women who were advanced in pregnancy, sliced open their bellies so that their babies dropped out, and then threw their living children to wild dogs.

Before leaving this section I would like to comment on the first element of the above torture; that of sewing up victims in animal skins. This procedure is the only element required for the bull's-hide torture that was practised in India many years ago. The victim, tightly bound hand and foot, was sewn up in the newly skinned hide of a buffalo. As the hide gradually dried in the full power of the tropical sun, it contracted and drew with it the flesh of the victim, causing a prolonged and agonising death. A similar method of torture, using the well stretched skin of a freshly killed sheep, was practised by the Mahrattas with the same devastating results. As with the bull's-hide torture, putrefaction speedily set in and combined with the hunger and thirst, death eventually came, but not until after interminable agony had been suffered by the victim.

PLATE 10.

Crucifixion

Crucifixion

Crucifixion is one of the oldest tortures known to man and was practised by the Phoenicians, Scythians, Greeks, Romans, Persians and Carthagenians. Different races at different periods of time in history used various forms of the wooden cross to crucify their victims. The form of the cross which perhaps most people are familiar with is the one pictured in the illustration (see PLATE 10.) and consists of a short piece of timber attached horizontally to a longer upright stake. The usual custom was for the upright stake of the cross to be fastened firmly into the ground before the execution, and not, as is widely believed, carried to the site by the prisoner; the prisoner, usually after being scourged, was only responsible for carrying the cross-beam of the crucifix to the place of his execution.

When the prisoner's final destination was reached, he was stripped naked and usually forced to lay himself upon the ground, face upward, with his arms stretched out along the length of the cross-beam, (there are of course variations to this procedure as illustrated in PLATE 10., where the victim, in this case, has been crucified upside-down). The procedure for fastening the victim to the cross-beam was of two types; in some cases rope was used to bind the arms, in others the sole fastenings were long nails driven through the palm of each hand. The victim was then raised in that agonising position, to be fixed to the upright stake with either nails or rope. In cases where nails were used to fix the victim to the cross-beam the weight of the body was supported by a large peg attached to the upright stake. This was done in order to prevent the weight of the prisoner's body tearing the flesh of his hands away from the cross-beam, thereby allowing him to drop. In cases where each foot was to be nailed to the upright, the victim's feet were nailed by a long nail driven through the instep and sole of each foot.

The suffering of the crucified prisoners was unutterably agonizing and could be increased a hundredfold by the maliciousness of their persecutors. Keeping the victims of crucifixion alive by giving them food and drink allowed the torturers to indulge in their sick pleasures over a period of days. The faces and breasts of the prisoners were often torn to pieces by hooked implements; sticks were thrust into and withdrawn from their anal or urethral passages, their bodies prodded with spears or pointed stakes, their legs broken by heavy blows. Whatever the case, the unfortunate prisoners suffered long, slow, and painful deaths.

PLATE 11.

Burned At The Stake

christians bound to Axelltrees pitched in the ground in Rowes and so burned.

Burned At The Stake

The prisoners pictured in the illustration taken from Samuel Clarke's martyrology of 1651 (see PLATE 11.), are once again the unfortunate victims of the emperor Nero who seems to have taken great delight in devising as many different modes of torture for his Christian prisoners, as his warped mind could generate. According to Clarke, Nero, apart from sewing up Christians in the skins of wild beasts, impaling them upon stakes, crucifying them, or burning them in public to furnish the evenings with bonfires: "Many he caused to be packed up in paper stiffened in molten wax, with a coat of searcloth about their bodies, bound upright to axletrees, many of which were pitch in the ground, and so set on fire at the bottom, to maintain light for Nero's night-sports in his gardens."

The antiquity of burning alive as a form of execution is established in the bible; "If a man abide not in me, he is cast forth as a branch, and is withered; and men gather, and cast them into the fire, and they are burned." The Babylonians and Hebrews used it as a method of execution for certain crimes and it is likely that in the early days of civilization nearly all countries practised some form of burning at the stake for executing their prisoners.

Burning at the stake was the favourite sentence for those found guilty of heresy by the Inquisition, who, in their infamous heyday, condemned thousands to the flames. It was also the preferred method throughout all the countries in Europe, regardless of their faith, for dealing with alleged sorcerers and witches. For centuries in Britain, burning at the stake had been a recognized form of execution for certain crimes. I will illustrate its barbarity by giving the reader an example of its use in the execution of the Lord Bishop of Gloucester, Dr. John Hooper, for the crime of heresy.

In 1555, at Gloucester, near a great elm tree by the college of priests, some 7,000 eager spectators watched, as Bishop Hooper knelt down and prayed in preparation for his execution. With a pound of gunpowder held in a bladder between his legs (a privilege granted to some to bring death more quickly) and the same quantity in bladders held under each arm, he was led to the stake. To secure him to the stake, three iron hoops had been brought to fasten around his neck, waist and legs. The iron hoop to fit around his waist was far too small but after a struggle it was eventually made to fit; he refused to have the other two hoops fitted.

Faggots and bundles of reeds were then placed around the stake, the Lord Bishop being given two bundles of reeds, of which he placed one bundle under each arm. The fire was then lit, but owing to the number of green faggots, it took some time before the reeds caught fire and even when they did light, the wind blowing in the wrong direction caused the flames to veer away from the Bishop.

A more vehement fire was lit and it was then that the bladders full of gunpowder exploded; unfortunately for the Bishop, they did not kill him but only compounded his suffering. His prayers and cries could be heard as his face turned black with flame and even as his cries diminished he was seen to beat his breast with both hands until one of his arms dropped off, the other arm continuing to move while the fat, water, and blood dripped out at his finger ends. Soon after, the whole lower part of his body being consumed by flame, the upper part of his body toppled over the iron hoop that restrained him and fell into the fire accompanied by the excited yells of the crowd. It took more than three quarters of an hour for the whole of this obnoxious process to be completed.

PLATE 12.

Impaling

christians Gored vpon stakes one End
Fastned in the Ground the other
Coming out of theyre mouthes

Impaling

Considered by many to be the cruelest method of torture ever to be conceived by the human mind (see **PLATE 12.**), impaling (as already mentioned), was a torture used by the emperor Nero upon his Christian prisoners. According to Samuel Clarke, this depraved monster would have his victims, "gored in length upon stakes, the one end fastened in the earth, the other coming out at their mouths."

However, in the history of this particular torture, Nero's name pales into insignificance when one considers the infamous career of Vlad III, (1431-1476), also known as, Vlad Tepes (Vlad the Impaler) or Vlad Dracula (Vlad son of the Dragon), who intermittently ruled an area of the Balkans called Wallachia. During his harsh reign no one was immune to Vlad's attention, whether it be women, children, peasants, great lords or invading armies. Vlad would torture thousands of his enemies at a time often arranging the stakes upon which they had been impaled in various geometric patterns. The most common pattern that he used, a ring of concentric circles, he would place on the outskirts of his targeted town or city. At least Vlad had some perverted respect for order; He would denote the rank of his enemies by impaling them on graduated lengths of stakes, the taller the stake the higher the rank the victim held.

The decaying corpses of Vlad's atrocities were often left for months and it is said that an army of invading Turks turned back in fear when they encountered thousands of rotting corpses impaled on the banks of the river Danube. Also, in 1461, Mohammed II, not a squeamish man by nature, was sickened by the sight that greeted him outside the city of Tirgoviste. What greeted Mohammed on that fateful day, and which is remembered in history as "the Forest of the Impaled," was the gruesome spectacle of twenty thousand impaled Turkish prisoners.

Vlad's usual method of impalement was to have a horse attached to each leg of the victim to enable a sharpened stake to be forced into the body. In order to ensure that the victim did not die too rapidly through shock, the end of the stake would be oiled and care taken not to make it come to too sharp a point. The aims of the process were to pass the stake up through the anus and out through the mouth but in many cases the stake would become obstructed or emerge through the chest or more commonly the neck. Variations of this procedure are recorded where Vlad had his victims impaled through the legs, arms, and skull and even upside down. Perhaps one of the more outrageous acts perpetrated by Vlad was to have infants impaled on stakes forced through their mothers' chests.

PLATE 13.

Thrown To Wild Beasts

Thrown To Wild Beasts

Christians were regarded as common criminals by the Romans because they refused to participate in the rites of the state religion or to recognise the divinity of the emperor and were, therefore, guilty of the heinous crimes of sacrilege and treason. They along with prisoners found guilty of murder, arson, and other serious offences became the lunchtime amusement at the Gladiatorial games.

A day at the arena would begin something like this: An elaborate procession, including all the combatants and led by the sponsor would take place. In Rome during the imperial period, the sponsor of the games was usually the emperor or in the provinces it was a high ranking magistrate. The morning events might include such things as mock fights and animal displays; the displays featured trained animals that performed tricks or, more often than not, contained staged hunts (venationes) in which exotic animals were pitted against each other or hunted and killed by the lowest rank of gladiator known as the 'bestiarii,' who were also, incidentally, responsible for the training of the animals. The lunch break, that preceded the afternoon programme of individual gladiatorial combats, was devoted to the executions of the criminals.

The public nature of the executions made it degrading as well as painful and it was hoped by the authorities that it would deter others from committing the same crimes that these pitiable creatures were being executed for. One form of execution carried out in the arena was 'damnatio ad bestias,' in which the condemned prisoners were cast into the arena with ferocious animals (see PLATE 13.), or were made to participate in dramatic re-enactments of mythological tales in which the actors *really did* die.

The Romans were not the only ones with a penchant for throwing their prisoners to wild animals; many tyrants used this mode of torture to execute their victims. Another man, whose case like that our old friend Vlad, belongs to the realms of psychopathology and who, along with most of the other tyrants in history, should have been shut up in a mental asylum, is that of Ivan IV, better known as Ivan the Terrible.

Ivan ruled with a rod of iron, and with sadistic pleasure he gloated over the suffering of his subjects. 20,000 inhabitants of Novgorod were tortured and murdered on his orders. He saw his subjects' flesh cut to ribbons by the fiendish 'knut' (a vicious type of whip banned in Russia in 1845); he watched as they were racked, burnt alive, or thrown to the wild animals that Ivan kept especially for that purpose.

PLATE 14.

Boiling To Death

St. Iohn put into a Cauldron of Boiling oile

Boiling To Death

Boiling to death (see PLATE 14.) is a very old form of execution repeatedly referred to in ancient literature. The victim, bound hand and foot, would be immersed in a huge cauldron filled with water, oil (as used in the illustration), or tallow. The liquid in the cauldron was brought to boiling point and the victim was thrown, more often as not headfirst, into the boiling contents. If the executioner was particularly vicious and wished to prolong the agony of the victim, the contents of the cauldron would be gradually brought to the boil with the victim immersed in the liquid as shown in PLATE 14., although I doubt very much that the victim would look quite as calm as he does there!

The execution of Richard Roose which took place at Smithfield, in 1530, is an instance of this horrific form of execution. Roose, a cook for the Bishop of Rochester's household, was responsible for poisoning seventeen persons, two of whom died. By a retrospective law, Roose was found guilty of high treason and condemned to be boiled to death without the benefit of the clergy.

PLATE 15.

flagellation

Flagellation

Over the years many types of whips, rods, and even cudgels have been used in the act of flagellation and it has often been viewed as a judicial punishment rather than an act of torture. Depending on the severity of blows, the period of punishment and the condition of the victim, there is a very thin line between the two concepts, especially when one examines the nature of some of the instruments used.

For a victim who has received a beating with whips loaded with metal balls or hooks, the Russian knut, the cat-o'-nine-tails, the bastinado of Eastern nations or, if historically correct, white-hot metal rods; I do not see how any of these means of punishment can be interpreted as anything else but torture. Flagellation when compounded with the act of stringing the victim up by the hair (see PLATE 15.) is torture, regardless of what instrument of flagellation is used.

The practice of flagellation was, and still is, so universal that complete volumes on the subject have been written. I will therefore give only one example of its more barbarous use:

On May 8, 1811, the Honourable Arthur William Hodge (not so honourable when you read his story), was executed in the British West Indies for the whipping to death of his slave Prosper. Unfortunately, Prosper was not the only slave to suffer Hodge's murderous cruelty. A paper in connection with the case and read in the House of Commons, told the following revolting story about Hodge's mistreatment of his slaves.

Hodge employed a slave called Welcome as a slave-hunter to pursue and capture runaway Negroes. In

January, 1806, Welcome made three unsuccessful expeditions to capture runaway slaves and each time on his return, Hodge had him cart-whipped. The wounds from one severe flogging were still unhealed when the next whipping took place. In consequence, by the third time Welcome was beaten, his body could take no more punishment and he died.

Shortly after the death of Welcome, Hodge was responsible for the death of two female slaves attached to his establishment. He accused the cook and a washer woman of attempting to poison his wife and children. He poured boiling water down their throats, had them stripped and severely cart-whipped, and then sent them in this bloody state to work in the fields.

During the following two years, 1807 and 1808, the cart-whip was seldom idle. Slave after slave was whipped to death, under Hodge's orders, for the most trifling offences or for no offences at all. One witness testified at Hodge's trial that in the three years that he had been with Hodge, at least sixty slaves had been buried and only one of those had died of natural causes.

PLATE 16.

Thrown From Cliffs

Som Throne Downe From Rocks And Broken to Peeces.

Thrown From Cliffs

This was a convenient method of execution, popular among savage and primitive races, where precipices or rocks were readily available for its employment. It was a prescribed legal method of execution in ancient Rome as indicated by Samuel Clarke's illustration (see PLATE 16.). It was the fate of Manlius Capitolinus (a patrician of the Roman Republic; consul in 392 BC.), who was condemned as a rebel and thrown from the Tarpeian Rock. Other notable victims of this mode of execution were the emperor Zeno, the mathematician Putuanius, the famous author Aesopus, and Perilaus, the inventor of the ingenious instrument of torture called the brazen bull (see page 63).

The obvious torture associated with this method of execution was the terrible suffering endured by the victims with broken limbs if they were not killed outright by the fall. The victims would lay helpless for days until they literally starved to death; there are reports that some of the victims, out of sheer desperation, would actually eat the flesh of their own arms. In 1655, one victim of this method of execution, Pietro Simond of Angrogno, had his neck and heels tied together before his execution took place. On being thrown from a precipice the unfortunate man was caught in a tree, and although perhaps not so badly injured as some of those who had gone before him, he remained in the tree until he eventually died of starvation.

PLATE 17.

Hung Upon A Gibbet

Hanging And Gibbeting

"When the English gave up boiling people alive they took happily to hanging ..... This was not for any humane reason. Until the present day, such motives have always been out of place on any question of capital punishment ..... Old methods were only changed because they eventually proved too troublesome, too expensive or not painful enough."[1].

No other mode of execution has been so embedded in the British psyche as that of hanging. The Anglo-Saxon word for gallows is 'gala,' certainly a very apt expression, because by the end of the seventeenth century hanging days at Tyburn had become like a modern day Bank Holiday with drunken, cheering, gin-swilling mobs, watching the victims progress to the 'Three-legged mare' (Tyburn Gallows).

The triangular gallows at Tyburn was responsible for many popular expressions still used in the English language today. "To land in the cart," means to take a trip to Tyburn if you do something wrong; "To pull someone's leg," although having a different meaning today, originated from the humane act of pulling on the victim's legs, performed by the friends of the hung victim, to speed up the onset of death. The phrase "turned off" originated from the victim being 'turned off' the ladder in those places that still used that primitive method of hanging. Even our superstitions are not immune from the influence of hanging; the English superstition about not walking under a ladder stems from the fact that anyone who walked under the gallows' ladder was due to be hanged.

1. John Deane Potter, *The Fatal Gallows Tree*, 1965, p.9

In the middle ages, no distinction was made between hanging and gibbeting (see PLATE 17.) and the two terms were literally interchangeable. In plate seventeen the victim has been hung by the neck to slowly strangle to death, and this is what most people understand by the word 'hanging'. In the next plate (see PLATE 18.), the victims have been suspended by their legs and left to die of starvation and this is more in line with what we understand by the term gibbeting.

In medieval times a male victim would sometimes be hung by the neck, cut down and disembowelled (which usually included castration) and then chopped into pieces to be displayed on spikes around various parts of the city. At other times the whole corpse would be hung on a hook on another gallows, consisting of an upright with an arm running at right angles to the top (see PLATE 17.), called a gibbet. When a body was gibbeted it was meant as a warning to other potential miscreants and it was left in plain sight to be picked at by crows and other scavengers until it completely rotted and fell too pieces.

Occasionally, like the people pictured in plate eighteen, the victim would be gibbeted alive. In the thirteenth century, Sir Thomas Turberville who acted as a secret agent for the French, was condemned to be hanged alive by an iron chain. On 6 October 1295, he rode, hood about his head and feet tied beneath the belly of his horse, from the Tower of London to the Great Hall of Westminster. There, Sir Robert Brabazun condemned him to be drawn and then hanged by an iron chain until his life had expired.

Sir Thomas was then placed on a fresh oxhide and drawn by horse across the cobbled streets of London to his place of execution. The oxhide was not supplied for any humanitarian purpose but to ensure that Sir Thomas did not die too quickly; they did not want him to arrive at the scaffold already half dead from being dragged over rough terrain.

PLATE 18.

Hung By The Legs Until Dead

Being drawn along the ground is a torture in its own right and will be discussed more fully later on in this book. It is also a component part of the phrase 'hanged, drawn and quartered,' which is somewhat inverted and should read 'drawn, hanged and quartered.'

For centuries hanging was only a part of the torturous punishment inflicted on those poor wretches who fell foul of the law and were sentenced to be 'hanged, drawn and quartered.' The penalty was actually sevenfold in nature:

1. The condemned man shall be drawn to the gallows.

2. He is there to be hanged by the neck and let down alive.

3. His bowels are to be taken out.

4. And while he his still alive they are to be burnt.

5. His head is to be cut off.

6. His body is to be divided into four parts.

7. His head and quarters are to be placed where our lord the king shall direct.

Before anyone gets the idea that psychopathic tyrants are the exclusive property of other countries, Henry VIII is estimated to have hanged 72,000 of his subjects while on the throne, nearly 10,000 of these executions taking place at Tyburn. During a rebellion that broke out after the dissolution of the monasteries and which spread as far as Yorkshire, Henry's orders to quell it were, "You must cause such dreadful execution upon a good number of inhabitants, hanging them on trees quartering them and setting their heads and quarters in every town as should be a fearful warning."

Of course not all psychopathic tyrants are male. Henry's daughter, Mary, aptly nicknamed 'Bloody' Mary, shared her father's cruel nature. In her short reign she accounted for 1,400 deaths at Tyburn alone and there is very little doubt that if she had lived longer she may well have equalled, if not surpassed, her father's brutal tally.

PLATE 19.

Decapitation

Decapitation

Although this method of execution was not considered to involve any form of torture this was not always the case. If the head was severed from the body with one single blow then death would be instantaneous, but to be certain this occurred, one could only rely on automatic appliances such as the guillotine, or the even earlier Halifax gibbet (see below) to see that the job was done properly. For a swordsman (see PLATE 19.), or an axe man, to achieve this feat, they would require a skill that came from long practice combined with great strength and a keen bladed implement. Unfortunately there are many instances when this did not happen.

In July 1663, Lord Russell, who was considered too important to hang, was beheaded by Jack Ketch in Lincolns Inn Fields. Ketch was so clumsy and inept when wielding the axe that it would be more accurate to say that the axe crushed its way through the flesh and bone rather than cutting or slicing it. It took Ketch three or four attempts before he removed Lord Russell's head.

Another victim of Ketch's butchery, also considered too noble to hang, was the Duke of Monmouth. After his unsuccessful rebellion in the West Country, the Duke was sentenced to be beheaded by Ketch. He had heard of Ketch's bungling of Lord Russell's execution and gave Ketch six guineas to do a better job. He had also given his servant another purse of guineas to hand to Ketch if the execution went well. Needless to say Ketch did not earn the extra guineas. After four strokes Ketch had still not beheaded Lord Monmouth and was finally compelled to use a knife to sever his head.

If you think Ketch was bad - it is recorded in 'Memoirs of the Sansons', that when De Thou was executed in Paris, it took the executioner eleven blows before De Thou's head became separated from his body.

The Halifax gibbet, mentioned above, took a little of the barbarity out of decapitation by ensuring that the head of the victim was removed with one swift blow. It was used in Halifax in Yorkshire during the first half of the seventeenth century because the people of Halifax could not find anyone to act as hangman. The inventor of this killing machine was, with the Church's usual enthusiasm for executions, a local friar, and consisted of a heavy blade, placed between two tall supports. The blade, being positioned directly over the neck of the victim, was attached to a rope and then raised by the use of horses. When the blade reached the top of the tall supports the rope was cut with an axe and the force of gravity served to do the rest of the grisly task. Although more humane than hanging, in 1650, after 50 executions had been carried out by the friars invention, the Lord Bailiff of Halifax, was warned in no uncertain terms by the government of the day, that if he carried out anymore executions in this manner, he would be in big trouble. It appears that the British establishment, with its usual callousness, preferred slow strangulation rather than a quick and merciful death for its thieves and murderers.

PLATE 20.

Broiled Alive

Broiled Alive

Broiling alive is a very similar technique to that of roasting alive: The only distinction I make for the benefit of this present work, is that in the method of broiling, there is an intermediary between the victim and the flames; in the case of Samuel Clarke's illustration (see PLATE 20.), the gridirons heated by the flames from below.

Perhaps one of the most fiendishly ingenious inventions conceived by one man's warped mind, and using the broiling method of torture, was the 'brazen bull,' which stood in the temple of the first Phalaris (c. 570 - 554 B.C.), tyrant of Acragas (Agrigentum) in Sicily. Perilaus of Athens was the inventor of this diabolical instrument of torture and knowing the reputation for cruelty of the tyrant Phalaris brought it to Phalaris for inspection and to explain the ingenuity of the torture that it was designed to produce.

The apparatus consisted of a life size replica of a bull, constructed of metal, and hollow on the inside: A trap-door was set in the back of the bull to allow for the ingress and egress of the unfortunate victim. Perilaus explained to Phalaris that the culprit was to be shut up inside the bull and a fire kindled underneath. By means of an ingenious arrangement of flutes in the bull's nostrils, the agonized roars and screams of the victim would be transformed into the melodious lowing of a bull.

Phalaris, asked Perilaus to climb inside the bull and imitate the cries of a tortured man to prove that the bull would emit the charming music that Perilaus claimed it would. No sooner was Perilaus inside the bull than Phalaris shut the aperture and had a fire kindled beneath it. "Take that," said Phalaris, "as the only recompense such a piece of art is worth, and chant us the first specimen of the charming notes of which you are the inventor!"[1]

Rather than have Perilaus die inside the bull and thereby contaminate it, Phalaris had him removed and thrown off a cliff (see page 52). If it is any consolation to Perilaus; Phalaris was eventually overthrown in a general uprising and broiled alive in the same brazen bull.

---

1. Lucian *Works*.

PLATE 21.

Peine forte et dure

Peine forte et dure

Peine forte et dure or pressing to death (see PLATE 21.) basically involved placing heavy weights upon the victims' bodies until they were literally crushed to death.

The usual procedure was for the victim to be stripped of all clothing except for that covering his private parts, laid upon his back on the bare ground in a dark room, and his arms and legs tied with cords which were fastened to several parts of the room. Iron, stone, or lead weights, were placed upon his body until the victim could bear no more. The next day he was given three morsels of barley bread but no water; the following day he was given water and bread. This diet was continued in rotation until the victim finally died.

According to Luke Owen Pike in 'A History of Crime in England,' 1873, it was customary for the English to place a sharp piece of timber under the back of the victim to hasten his death, (how kind!).

There were variations to the above procedure: In 1658, when Major Strangeways was condemned to peine forte et dure, a heavy piece of iron was placed at an angle above his heart and the attendants at his execution threw their own bodyweights upon it. The major was mercifully dead within eight to ten minutes.

In the early part of the eighteenth century fifteen new condemned cells were built at Newgate prison on the east side of the Press Yard. The Press Yard had nothing to do with journalism - it was the place where prisoners who refused to plead were pressed to death with heavy weights.

It may be wondered why anyone in their right mind would suffer this terrible torture in order not to plead. One reason, of course, may have been that the prisoner was physically unable to do so, because he was deaf and dumb. This problem didn't appear to bother the judges of the time though, as the following account will testify:

In 1735, at Nottingham assizes, an alleged murderer, for failing to plead, was pressed to death. This sentence was carried out despite the fact that several witness statements corroborated the fact that the man had been deaf and dumb from birth. In fairness to the judges (if one possibly can be), it would not be the first time that a defendant had tried to avoid making a plea on the grounds that they were deaf and dumb.

In 1740, at Kilkenny assizes, Mathew Ryan was tried for highway robbery. By pretending that he was dumb and could not plead, Ryan hoped to stand a better chance in the case brought before the court. However, it was decided that his affliction was simulated and he was told by the judges that the law now called for peine forte et dure. The judges actually tried to be compassionate in his case, by deferring the actual sentence to a future date in the hope that Ryan would consider the gravity of his situation. When he was again brought before the judges he still stubbornly refused to plead, gambling on the premise that the judges might eventually believe that he actually *was* dumb. The gamble didn't pay off; the court at last pronounced the dreadful sentence and two days later Ryan was executed in the public market-place. It was not until the weights were being placed upon Ryan's body that he finally spoke, begging to be hung rather than suffer the terrible agony he was going through. Unfortunately for Ryan, it was too late!

PLATE 22.

Stoning

Stoning

Because of its obvious convenience, stoning is a very antiquated form of torture. In the Old Testament it was the approved method of execution for blasphemy, heresy, idolatry, adultery and many more alleged criminal acts. In historical times, in Judaism, the laws for stoning dictated that two reputable people must have witnessed the offence and they must also witness the actual stoning. In Judaism, stoning has long been abolished; unfortunately however, it is still carried out today in many countries with Muslim majorities. Stonings, with and without legal proceedings, are reported to have been carried out in Sudan, Saudi Arabia and the United Arab Emirates. The Jawa Report, March 18 2006, said that even in a 'moderate' Muslim country like Indonesia almost 50% of the people support stoning for adultery, while a more disturbing survey carried out in August 2009 (Pew Report, page 3), found that 83% of Pakistanis believe that adulterers should be stoned.

On 27 October 2008, the BBC news reported that in Somalia, a young girl called Aisho Ibrahim Dhuhulow, was buried up to her neck at a football stadium and then stoned to death in front of more than 1,000 people. The stoning occurred after she allegedly pleaded guilty to adultery in a Sharia court in Kismayo, a city controlled by Islamist insurgents. According to the insurgents she wanted Shari'ah law to apply; however, other sources state (BBC news 4 November 2008), that the victim had been crying for mercy and had to be forced into the hole before being buried up to her neck in the ground. Amnesty International later learned that the girl was in fact 13 years old and had been arrested by Al-Shabab militia after she had been reported being gang-raped by three men.

Another instance of stoning was reported in the 'Daily Mail,' 14 December 2009. Mohamed Abukar Ibrahim was accused of adultery by the Hizbul Islam Militant Group: Somalian villagers were forced to watch Mohamed being stoned to death.

PLATE 23.

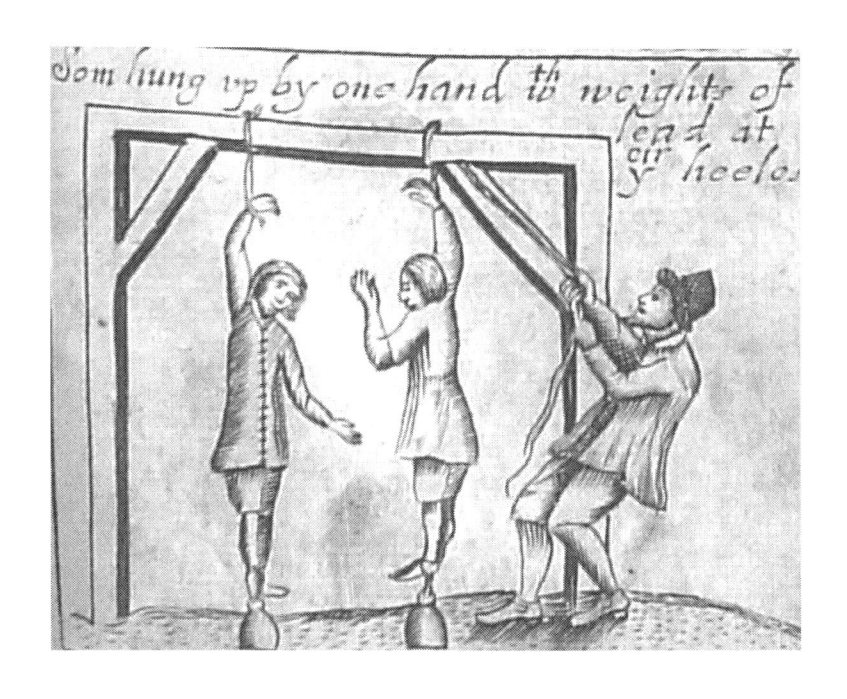

Suspended By One Arm

Suspended By One Arm

This method of torture (see PLATE 23.), is similar to one that was used on the orders of Sir Thomas Picton, late Governor of Trinidad, in order to extract a confession from a young native girl named Louise Calderon.

In the December of 1801, the eleven year old Louise Calderon was living with Pedro Ruiz as his mistress. Carlos Gonzalez, a friend Ruiz, visited the house often and started an affair with Louise behind Ruiz's back. Not content with stealing Ruiz's mistress, he stole some of Ruiz's money as well. Louise Calderon was suspected of being an accomplice to the theft and along with Gonzalez was arrested by the police. She refused to admit complicity in the theft, so Sir Thomas Picton gave orders for her to be tortured.

She was taken to a room where the torture was prepared. Here she was suspended from the ceiling by her left wrist; her right hand and right foot were tied together behind her back and her left foot was rested on a wooden spike fixed into the floor. In this torturous position the girl remained for three quarters of an hour. She had already fainted before she was taken down, but her ordeal was not yet over, the following day the torture was repeated.

Failing to get a confession from the girl, her feet were placed in irons that were fastened to the wall of a prison cell. The cell into which she was put had sloping side walls like that of a garret, and the irons by which she was restrained, were so positioned, so as not to allow her to raise herself upright. In these intolerable conditions she was incarcerated for a full eight months.

The details of this cold-bloodedly inhuman act

came to light at the trial of Sir Thomas Picton, who, on February 24, 1806, was convicted for the torture of Louise Calderon.

PLATE 24.

Clubbed To Death

Clubbed To Death

This barbaric form of execution (see PLATE 24.), was practised in the Sandwich Islands where criminals were either clubbed to death or strangled with a rope. The use of clubs to beat people with is universal and examples can be found even up to the present day, where the police forces of different countries use clubs to beat protesters with during civil unrest. Usually, fatalities resulting from this use are quite rare, but they do happen.

During a period of civil unrest in Moldova in April, 2009, which began after the announcement of preliminary election results, film footage was taken by 'Radio Free Europe,' of demonstrators being dragged away and beaten with clubs by what appeared to be plain-clothes police officers. One protester, 23 year old Valeria Boboc, died in police custody. The police claim he died of smoke inhalation from the riot, but his family insists that he was beaten to death by the police, his body being full of contusions.

Clubbing to death as a method of execution is mentioned in the 'Legend of Felicitas and the Seven Holy Brothers,' where two of the brothers, Felix and Philip, were executed in this way. The legend tells of Felicitas and her seven sons being brought before Publius, the Prefect of Rome, because of their professed Christianity and refusal to worship pagan gods. Before Publius, they adhered to their family religion and were therefore handed over to four judges who condemned the seven brothers to various modes of death, with Felicitas being forced to watch her sons gruesome executions. Januaris, the eldest was scourged to death; Felix and Philip were clubbed to death; Silvanus was thrown headlong down a precipice; and the three youngest brothers, Alexander, Vitalis and Martialis were beheaded. Still refusing to act against her conscience and renounce Christianity, Felicitas was executed four months later.

Although the Romans are known to have used all the methods of execution mentioned above, I cannot find any evidence to support the fact that this particular family ever existed. The Catholic Church obviously believe in their existence as the whole family have been canonized, the mother being known as, Saint Felicitas of Rome, (c. 101- 165), who is buried in the catacomb of Maximus on the Via Silania, beside St. Silvanus. I have my doubts; the story, as interesting as it is, could almost be a re-write of the story of the Maccabee family related earlier in this book.

Legends aside, one evidential example of this cruel method of execution is that Ivan the Terrible's son had his brains bashed out with a club. Readers may not be surprised to learn that it was Ivan himself who wielded the club.

PLATE 25.

Sharp Implements Forced Underneath Fingernails

> Som had sharp reeds thrust
> under theyr nailes And
> other parts of their Body

Sharp Implements Forced Underneath Fingernails

In the illustration (see PLATE 25.), sharp reeds have been forced under the victim's fingernails. Whether the offending implements are reeds, pins, nails or bamboo slivers, this type of torture has been used extensively throughout history.

Pitcairn's 'Criminal Trials' (1833), gives an account of the torture of Doctor Fian (alias John Cunningham), suspected of being a sorcerer. Notwithstanding the other tortures that Cunningham underwent, two needles were driven up to their heads, under every one of his nails.

General Knox, referring to atrocities committed by the Bolshevists during 1918-19, said that at Blagoveschensk, gramophone needles were found thrust underneath the finger nails of the mutilated corpses of officers and soldiers from Torbolof's detachment. 'The Times' (March 23 1928), reported that "driving splinters under the fingernails" was "a favourite device" of the Chinese Communists to extort money out of prosperous tradesmen.

One only has to search the internet to realize how prevalent, relatively recent cases of this method of torture are. Below are just a few examples:

Don Luce, in a statement made at a conference sponsored by Amnesty International of the USA, held in New York on April 30 1973, identified the 'bamboo sliver torture' while referring to political prisoners held in the jails of the Saigon government. He stated that (from personal interviews with Vietnamese who had undergone such torture), that slivers of bamboo were forced under the prisoners' fingernails. A variation to this torture was where a pin with a feather attached to it was used under the fingernails of the victim and then an electric fan was turned on to rotate the pin and increase the agony of the sufferer.

'Tamilnet,' Saturday 31 March, 2001, reported that Sri Lanka's Supreme Court granted leave for a Tamil girl from Kayts in Jaffna to proceed with a fundamental rights petition claiming that she was repeatedly tortured by the police. She said that one of the tortures that she underwent while in custody was to be held down flat onto a table by four policemen while another four policemen pricked paper pins under the nails of her fingers. When the pins were under her fingernails, the policemen simultaneously moved the pins in and out of her nails causing the Petitioner unbearable pain; at the same time copious amounts of blood oozed out of the pricked places.

The United Nations 'Special Rapporteur on Torture' 2006, reports that two thirds of the torture cases listed in China, were tortures of Falun Gong adherents. Falun Gong is a spiritual discipline whose followers have been persecuted by the Chinese government since 1999. In an internet document dated 17 May 2008, it is claimed that as part of a series of tortures inflicted upon Falun Gong followers, their fingertips were pierced with pins and bamboo nails were hammered under their fingernails.

PLATE 26.

Executed By Saw

Som were sawed asunder in the midle

Executed By Saw

Sawing as a method of torture and execution for the condemned was used in Europe under the Roman Empire, in the Middle East and in parts of Asia. The roman Emperor Caligula was said to be particularly fond of ordering this method of torture.

According to Samuel Clarke, Sapores, King of Persia, had a Christian Bishop named Simeon executed. A little while later, the Queen of Persia fell ill; the consequence of this coincidence was that Simeon's two sisters were executed in the cruel manner pictured overleaf (see PLATE 26.), after being accused of causing the Queen's sickness by sorcery. Clarke says of this incident:

"About this time the Queen fell very sick, upon which occasion the wicked Jews and Magicians accused two of Simeon's sisters, which were godly virgins, that by charms and enchantments had procured it to revenge the death of Simeon: This accusation being believed, they were both condemned, and with a Saw cut in sunder by the middle, whose quarters were hung upon stakes, the Queen going betwixt them, thinking thereby to be freed of her sickness."

The method of execution illustrated by Clarke (if it is accurate), was not the usual way that this type of execution was carried out in Europe or in Asia. The prescribed method in Europe, under the Roman Empire, was for the condemned person to be hung upside-down and then sawn down the middle, starting at the groin. This was a particularly nasty way of carrying out the execution as the victim's brain received a continuous supply of blood in spite of the severity of the bleeding. It was done in order to increase the suffering of the condemned person by ensuring he or she would remain completely conscious until the saw severed the major blood vessels of their abdomen.

In Asia, it was usual for the victim to be restrained while standing upright and the sawing started at the head. Whatever the procedure it must have been an agonizing death for the victim: Can you imagine the pain caused by the teeth of a large saw blade being drawn slowly back and forth across *your own* flesh and bone?

A peculiar method of torture, using a 'sawing' technique, was developed by the French Huguenots in their persecution of the Catholics. It consisted of drawing the victim's body along the length of a secured rope. The victim was stripped naked, laid lengthwise along a tightly stretched hard-fibred or wire rope, and then dragged backwards and forwards with a sawing motion to allow the rope to cut into the victims body. During this agonizing torture, the rope cut the flesh of the victim right down to the bone.

PLATE 27.

Tearing Of Skin

Som had all their flesh torne with the Clawes of wild Beasts

Tearing Of Skin

The specific method of torture pictured overleaf (see PLATE 27), i.e. tearing the skin with the claws of wild beasts, is mentioned in Samuel Clarke's martyrology under 'the tenth persecutions of the Christians' which began in 308 A.D.

In Alexandria, according to Clarke, the Bishop Phileas said that because of their faith, Christians were subjected to numerous tortures; one being that their persecutors, "scratched them with the claws of wilde beasts." One of the victims of this torture was a twelve year old Portuguese girl named Eulalia. She enraged a judge by professing her Christianity and refusing to bow down before Pagan Gods. As a result of this, she first had her joints pulled out and then her skin was torn to the bone by the use of claws taken from wild beasts. Her persecutors then burned her breasts with flaming torches and set fire to her long hair before she mercifully died.

Another Christian martyr, a Spaniard called Vincentius, had the skin of his body torn, not with the claws of wild beasts, but with iron combs whose teeth had been filed to very sharp points. Iron combs were also used during the torture of Apphianus on the orders of the tyrant Maximinus. Apphianus's feet were wrapped in cotton that had been soaked in oil and then set on fire: While his feet were burning, Apphianus was hung up in the air so that his torture would strike terror in those witnessing it. During his excruciatingly painful torture, while the flesh of his feet dropped off like melted wax, his tormenters tore the skin on his ribs with iron combs until his body became one swelling mass.

The Lydians had an instrument full of sharp points, which they used like a comb, to tear the skin of their victims during torture, and the Jews used a harrow in much the same way. A particularly disturbing case, where a harrow was used as an instrument of torture to tear the skin of the victim, is reported in Pitcairn's Trials.

In 1589, Magnus Andersoune, Johnne Andersoune and James Crawfurd, were charged with the torture of a young girl. The girl, Margaret Gairner, was accused by the three of stealing a purse of money from Crawford. In order to gain a confession from her, the trio forced the girl's fingers through the holes or perforations through which harrows are thrust, thereby causing a great deal of tearing to the skin on the girl's fingers. Still unable to gain a confession, the despicable trio burnt her upon the back, shoulders, and under the armpits with red hot tongs and in this agonizing state, left her tied and helpless, without food or water, for two whole days.

One of the most fiendish instruments ever designed for tearing and mutilating the skin of the victim is the 'Pear of Anguish.' Used during the Middle Ages, this pear shaped device, consisted of four leaves that slowly separated from each other as the torturer turned the screw at the top. Varying in size and adornment to differentiate between anal, vaginal, and oral use, it was inserted in the vagina for torturing women who had conducted a miscarriage; into the anus of men considered to be Homosexuals and in to the mouths of those considered to be liars or blasphemers. It was the torturer's prerogative whether to just badly tear the skin of the victim or to expand the 'pear' to its full extent and totally mutilate the targeted area. However, this torture as terrible as it was, rarely caused death and was often used as part of a serial torture.

PLATE 28.

Insect Torture

Som had their naked bodies
Anointed with hony - then
Hung up in baskets to be
Devoured with wasps and flies.

Insect Torture

The insect torture pictured (see PLATE 28.), was inflicted upon Marcus Arethusa, a Christian Bishop of a Roman province in Syria, on the orders of Flavius Claudius Julianus (born AD 332). Julian was the nephew of the first Christian Emperor Constantine and although brought up in the Christian religion he attempted to destroy it and revive Hellenism. For this reason, when he became emperor in AD 360, he was known as Julian the Apostate.

Julian, ordered Marcus Arethusa to rebuild a heathen temple, which the Bishop, by the command of Constantine, had raised to the ground. To avoid doing this the Bishop fled the city but soon returned when he discovered that the Christian people within the city would be made to pay for his departure. Julian put the Bishop through several tortures before (in the words of Samuel Clarke), "they put him into a basket, anointed him with honey and broth, and so hung him abroad in the heat of the sun, to be meat for wasps and flies to feed upon."

In India, tying a prisoner to a tree and smearing his face with honey to attract red ants was a popular form of torture, but perhaps one of the most revolting forms of insect torture to ever crawl out of the cesspit of the human mind, was known as 'Torture of the Boats.' This unique and terrible form of torture is said by Plutarch to have been the manner in which Mithridates was put to death by Artaxerxes, the King of Persia (465 BC - 424 BC). According to Plutarch, it took seventeen days for Mithridates to die after suffering unimaginable agony. The torture was designed as follows:

Mithradates was forced to lay on his back in a small boat, his head, hands and feet, all projecting over the sides. A second boat, exactly of the same size as the first, was placed over the top, thereby enclosing his body between the two boats but allowing his head, hands and feet to remain outside. Food was offered to Mithradates, but if he refused he was pricked and tormented until he complied. His mouth was then filled with a mixture of milk and honey, the excess being smeared about his face, and in this condition he was left in the full glare of the sun. In a short time the insects and flies settled upon his face and after hours and days of their incessant stinging and biting it drove Mithridates almost mad.

Unfortunately, this was not the only torment that he had to suffer; the accumulated excrement that gathered within the cavity of the two boats invariably became one sodden mass of stinking corruption. When Mithridates's death mercifully arrived, and the top boat was removed, what was witnessed was the dreadful sight of devoured flesh still visually pulsating with a swarm of scavenging vermin.

The insect torture is not just a thing of the past. On the 16 April 2009, the Washington Post published a memo that detailed torture techniques deemed legal by the Bush administration for use against terror suspects. (This article was also corroborated by a Timesonline article for 17 April 2009 entitled 10 'torture' techniques blessed by Bush). The insect torture specified was one of the tortures to be used on Abu Zubaydah, a high-ranking Al-Qaeda member. On the insect torture reported in the memo it was stated:

"You would like to place Zubaydah in a cramped confinement box with an insect. You have informed us that he appears to have a fear of insects. In particular, you would like to tell Zubaydah that you intend to place a stinging insect into the box with him. You would, however, place an harmless insect in the box. You have orally informed us that you would in fact place an harmless insect such as a caterpillar in the box with him."

On ClearHarmony Net for Saturday, 11 September, 2004, there is an article entitled '25 Torture Methods Jiang Zemin's Criminal Regime Uses to Persecute Falun Gong Practitioners' written by an ex-detainee of a forced labour camp. Number 12 on his list of tortures is "letting insects bite practitioners," it reads:

"During the insect and mosquito season, the victim is bound on a chair in a place where mosquitoes and insects are swarming. The victim is subjected to a great number of bites from these insects while immobilized and unable to scratch the bites or fend off the insects, leaving the victim susceptible to disease carried by the insects."

PLATE 29.

Dragged Along The Ground

> Som were tyed by the feet And halled throw Rough places till they were torne in peeces

Dragged Along The Ground

Hunrick, a tyrant of the vandals, ordered the Moors to transport nearly five thousand banished Christians into the wilderness. Pictured in the illustration (see PLATE 29.), is what happened to those Christians who were too weak to make the journey. Samuel Clarke writes:

"When any of the aged or tender children fainted, they were first punched forward with staves: Then were the Moors commanded to tie ropes to the feet of such as were unable to go, and to hale them thorow the rough places, so that first their garments were rent, then their flesh and their heads were dashed against the sharp edges of rocks, whereby many of them died."

The Emperor Tiberius was so feared because of the tortures that he inflicted upon his prisoners, that many of the guilty, rather than go to trial, would commit suicide the moment their transgressions were discovered. Can you blame them? This monster of cruelty, for the merest misdemeanour, would have both men and women dragged through the streets of Rome with iron hooks.

Other notorious torturers of the Roman Empire were Severus, Gallus, Decius and Valerianus who tortured anyone who refused to sacrifice to the imperial gods. One of the several tortures inflicted upon Christians and others accused or suspected of heresy was for the victims to be tied by the heels, attached to the tails of horses, and dragged along the ground until they were barely alive.

It must also be remembered, that being dragged along the ground to a place of execution, was one of the sevenfold penalties of being 'hanged, drawn and quartered' (see page 57). Before the introduction of the oxhide into this procedure, the unfortunate victim was dragged along the ground with no protection at all, for a journey up to three miles long (the distance between Newgate and Tyburn). One particularly nasty case of this procedure was recorded in 1177, when William Fitz Osbert, nicknamed Longbeard, was dragged to the gallows. As a calculated act of cruelty, sharp stones had been deliberately placed along the road by which he was to be drawn. Although intended to add to the victim's humiliation and suffering, it almost became an act of kindness, because by the end of the journey, William Fitz Osbert, was unconscious and so near to death, that he was probably incapable of feeling any further pain.

According to an article written by Recai Morkok and published on the internet in 2006: During the 1918 atrocities perpetrated by Armenian gangs upon the Turks, one of the methods of torture they used was to put people into sacks and drag them along the ground behind horses.

Ironically, a more recent example of this type of torture (although probably not so severe), is cited against the Turks on page 575 of the 'Human Rights Watch World Report.' It states:

"Respect for human rights deteriorated markedly in Turkey in 1991. In comparison with 1990, more people died in detention under suspicious circumstances ..... Torture continues to be used routinely in Turkey, largely in the political sections of police headquarters during the investigative phase of the case ....." It then reports a long list of tortures including, "dragging prisoners along the ground."

A yet more recent example of 'dragging along the ground,' was reported in the 'MailOnline,' for the 29 May, 2009. It concerned abuse allegations at the notorious Abu Ghraib prison in Baghdad between 2001 and 2005. A number of U.S. soldiers, were accused of abusing Iraqi prisoners; the article shows a photograph of one of the accused, 21 year-old Lynndie England, dragging a cowering prisoner along the ground attached to a dog lead. She, along with eleven other soldiers, was later convicted by a court martial of abusing inmates at the prison.

It is interesting to note that in the last two examples given; in one example, the offence is considered 'torture', in the other, it is considered 'abuse'. This begs the question - at what *point* does physical abuse become categorized as physical torture?

PLATE 30.

Suffocation

Suffocation

The illustration (see PLATE 30.), shows victims being suffocated by smoke during the tenth Persecution of the Christians, which, according to Samuel Clarke, began in 308 AD. He writes:

"In Thebaide, they hanged up women naked by one of their feet, the rest of their body hanging downwards, with many other sorts of punishment most cruel to be thought of: Some were bound to the boughs of trees, and had their members torn asunder, others were mangled with axes, some choked with smoak over a slow fire, some had their hands, ears, and feet cut off, others were scorched and broiled upon coals, yet not to death, but had the torment renued every day."

Also, according to Clarke, during the eighth Persecution of the Christians which began in 259 AD., under the reign of the Emperor Valerianus (Valerian I, reigned 253-260 AD.); "In Carthage three hundred Christians being brought before the President, were put to their choice either to offer sacrifice, or to go into a lime-kiln; whereupon by mutuall consent they all chose the lime-kiln, in which, with the smoak of the lime, they were smothered."

Another method of using smoke to suffocate Christians was used during the Persecution of the Waldenses by the President of Opede. He, apparently, declared war on Aix and Marseilles and in 1545 sent an army into Kofta which caused many of the residents to flee to the mountains. Many of the refugees were discovered by the soldiers hiding in caves: Setting fires at the mouths of these caves (see PLATE 31.), the soldiers left the people inside to die from smoke inhalation.

A modern day version of the torture of suffocating with smoke is reported to be in use in China today, in the Chinese government's alleged persecution of Falun Gong practitioners. Wang Bingwen, a thirty-three year old practitioner of Falun Gong, is said to have suffered this torture (along with many other tortures), after being detained in Qingdao Forced Labour Camp in August 2003. During his torture, two cigarettes were inserted into his nostrils and his mouth was covered to suffocate him. The suffocation and choking he experienced was said to be very painful.

Of course, there are other ways to suffocate a person other than by filling their lungs with smoke: A less sophisticated, but no less effective way, is simply to place a plastic bag over the victim's head. This seems to be the choice of many modern day torturers. Its leaves no physical evidence and it is very cheap to use. The Clear Harmony website gives a list of the tortures that the Falun Gong are allegedly subjected to in the Second Detention Centre and Forced Labour camp in Changchun; suffocation using a plastic bag, being just one of them:

"This is the type of torture that the Chinese police and prison guards (referred to as "torturers" from now on) frequently resort to when interrogating practitioners (about where they obtained the materials containing the facts about Falun Gong and who helped produce them). The torturers would seal a practitioner's head with a plastic bag to suffocate him while punching and kicking him, or shocking him with high-voltage stun batons. The feeling of being suffocated is horrific. The torturers would open the plastic bag after awhile and ask the victim if he is now willing to provide the information, which would surely cause his fellow practitioners to fall into the hands of the torturers. If the victim refuses to do so, the torturers would repeat the suffocation until the victim passes out or dies."

PLATE 31.

Christians suffocated with smoke

It is not only in modern-day China that this pernicious form of torture is used. The case I am about to relate took place in the Philippines as recently as May 2010, and was posted on the internet as 'Asian Human Right Commission - Urgent Appeal Case: AHRS-UAC-065-2010 14 May 2010.' The appended letter stated the following:

"Dear Friends

The Asian Human Rights Commission (AHRC) writes to inform you that a man arbitrarily arrested by the police in General Santos City was tortured while in custody for seven days. The police had him severely beaten, subjected him to suffocation using a plastic bag and burned his thumb with lit cigarettes."

The man subjected to this monstrous torture (torture has been criminal offence in the Philippines since November 2009), was 30 year-old Anuar T Hasim. Under section 4 of the "Anti-Torture Act of 2009," anyone found guilty of perpetrating the acts of torture that Hasim was subjected to, faces imprisonment for twelve to twenty years (although I wouldn't hold my breath that anyone will actually be brought to trial for this offence).

At the time of writing this book, another report of this appalling torture was given by 'Radio Free Europe.' On Wednesday, 16 June, 2010, United Nations official, Manfred Novak, said in Astana, that violence and torture exists in Kazakhstan's penitentiary system. He said he has medical proof of cases in which guards beat inmates with plastic bottles full of sand and placed plastic bags over inmates' heads to simulate suffocation.

PLATE 32.

Suffocation By Drowning

99

Suffocation By Drowning

The illustration (see PLATE 32.), refers to an incident that occurred during the Persecution of the Church in France, which began in 1524. From what I can gather from Clarke's text, the incident must have occurred sometime during the early part of the 1560's. He writes:

"At Tours, one hundred and forty were murdered and cast into the River; divers others were drowned, sparing neither man, woman, nor child. The President being suspected to favour them of the Religion was beaten with staves, stript to his shirt, hanged up by one foot, his head in the water up to the breast, and while he was yet living, they ript up his belly, pluck't out his guts, and threw them into the river; and sticking his heart upon the point of a Lance, they carried it about, saying, It was the heart of the heart of the President of the Huguenots."

In many ancient races, drowning sacrificial victims was a form of appeasement to the demons that supposedly inhabited the waters, thereby suppressing the demons' rage, which was demonstrated in the occurrence of furious storms.

In Rome, drowning was the chosen method of execution for bigamy and patricide, while in France, under Charles VI, it was the chosen method for sedition. Drowning seems to have been a favourite mode of execution for witches and sorcerers throughout the ages, and also acted as the 'Test of Innocence.'

The Babylonian Code of Hammurabi, prescribed that charges of sorcery and witchcraft should be tested in the following manner:

"If a man has laid a charge of witchcraft and has not justified it, he upon whom the witchcraft is laid shall go to the Holy River; he shall plunge into the Holy River and if the Holy River overcome him, he who accused him shall take to himself his house."

It is apparent from this that the people believed that the river would spare the innocent and drown the guilty. The Assyrians reversed this outcome, saying that the innocent would drown and that the guilty would float. This became the standard practice for the Christian accusers of medieval Europe.

When prisoners were accused of witchcraft they were stripped, bound hand and foot, tied around with a knotted rope, and thrown into the water. If the victims sank deep enough to drag the knot (which was tied some distance away from their bodies) under the water, then they were presumed innocent and they were pulled out. Unfortunately, many had already drowned by this time.

A form of water torture that had widespread use for minor offences, especially in relation to strumpets or scolds, was the ducking-stool. Popular in England and Scotland, the ducking-stool consisted of a chair or stool fixed to the end of a long pole. Operated either mechanically or by a number of people standing on the bank of the river or pond, the culprit seated in the chair, was lifted into the air and then ducked in the water. In many cases, to increase the suffering of the victim, a muddy or stinking pond was chosen for the location of the punishment. One of the last recorded instances of its use was reported in the 'London Evening Post' for April 27, 1745, when a woman for the offence of scolding was ducked in the river Thames to the delight of a crowd of two or three thousand people.

Water, or any liquid for that matter, used in torture as a means of suffocating by drowning, inspires terror and panic in the victim, even if it is not intended to be a fatal act. In earlier times, one crude method would be to simply thrust the victim's head into a bucket containing water, urine, vomit, or some other unpleasant liquid. More modern methods that simulate that same effect will be discussed later.

One seriously disturbed individual who preferred to use the cruder method of torture referred to above, was a gentleman the reader is already familiar with. The Honourable Arthur William Hodge (see page 49), had a propensity to treat the children of his Negro slaves in this manner. His favourite punishment was to have the children held by their feet, head hanging downwards, and then have them dipped into a tub of water until near to the point of suffocation. They were then lifted out to regain their breath before the torture was repeated.

Water torture was often used in combination with the rack (see page 121), when racking on its own proved ineffectual. Samuel Clarke describes a procedure called the 'aselli,' used by the Spanish Inquisition after racking, to create within the victim all the horrors of drowning:

"Yea sometimes they proceed to another kind of torture called the *A-Selli*, which is after this manner; There is a piece of timber somewhat hollowed on the top like a trough, about the middle whereof there is a sharp barre going a cross, whereon a mans back resteth that it cannot go to the bottom: its also placed so that his heels shall lie higher then his head: then is the naked Party laid thereon: His armes, thighs and legs bound with strong small cords, and wrested with short truncheons, till the cords pierce almost to the very bone. Then they take a thick fine lawn cloth, laying it over the Parties mouth as he lies upright on his back, so that it may stop his nostrils also; then taking a quantity of water, they poure it in a long stream like a threed, which falling from on high drives the cloth down into his throat, which puts the poor wretch into as great an Agony as any endure in the pains of death, for in this torture he hath not liberty to draw his breath, the water stopping his mouth and the cloth his nostrils, so that when the cloth is drawn out of the bottom of his throat, it draws forth blood with it, and a man would think that it tore out his very bowels. This is iterated as oft as the Inquisitors please, and yet they threaten him with worse torments if he confess not; and so he is returned to his prison again."

The description you have just read was published in 1651. Here is how a *civilized* country of today carries out the technique referred to above as 'aselli'. Now it is called 'waterboarding,' and was one of the 10 torture techniques deemed legal by the Bush administration (see page 88), to be used on Abu Zubaydah, a high-ranking Al-Qaeda member. It is interesting to compare the two descriptions:

"Finally, you would like to use a technique called the "waterboard" in this procedure, the individual is bound securely to an inclined bench, which is approximately four feet by seven feet.

The individual's feet are generally elevated. A cloth is placed over the forehead and eyes. Water is then applied to the cloth in a controlled manner. As this is done, the cloth is lowered until it covers both the nose and the mouth. Once the cloth is saturated and completely covers the mouth and nose, air flow is slightly restricted for 20 to 40 seconds due to the presence of the cloth. This causes an increase in carbon dioxide level in the individual's blood. This increase in the carbon dioxide level stimulates increased effort to breathe. This effort plus the cloth produces the perception of suffocation and incipient panic, i.e. *the perception of drowning.* (my italics)

The individual does not breathe any water into his lungs. During those 20 to 40 seconds, water is continuously applied from a height of twelve to twenty-four inches. After this period, the cloth is lifted, and the individual is allowed to breathe unimpeded for three or four full breaths. The sensation of drowning is immediately relieved by the removal of the cloth. The procedure may then be repeated. The water is usually applied from a canteen cup or small watering can with a spout.

You have orally informed us that this procedure triggers an automatic physiological sensation of drowning that the individual cannot control even though he may be aware that he is in fact not drowning. You have also orally informed us that it is likely that this procedure would not last more than twenty minutes in any one application.

We also understand that a medical expert with SERE experience will be present throughout this phase and that the procedures will be stopped if deemed medically necessary to prevent severe mental or physical harm to Zubaydah. As mentioned above Zubaydah suffered an injury during his capture. You have informed us that steps will be taken to ensure that this injury is not in any way exacerbated by the use of these methods and that adequate medical attention will be given to ensure that it will heal properly."

In spite of all the prescribed safeguards listed above, it is still *torture*. To put it in a nutshell, the 'waterboard,' like its predecessor the 'aselli' makes the victim feel like he's *drowning*.

PLATE 33.

Forced Ingestion Of A Liquid

Som had stinking water vineger & greafe poured downe theire throates

Forced Ingestion Of A Liquid

The Samuel Clarke illustration (see PLATE 33.), depicts 'forced ingestion,' one of the many tortures that the Christians in Africa suffered at the hands of an invading army of Vandals. According to Clarke, the Vandals tortured the Christians repeatedly for the sole purpose of extracting their gold and silver. Clarke writes of these tortures:

"The mouths of some they wrested open with iron, thrusting in stinking mire and dirt: Some they tormented by wresting their foreheads and legs with bow strings, till they crackt again: Into the mouths of others they poured sea-water, vinegar, with dregs of oyl and grease; and neither weakness of sex, nor respect of nobility, nor reverence of their Ministry, mitigated their mindes; yea their fury most abounded where appeared any dignity or worthinesse."

In relation to its suffocation aspect, forced ingestion is akin to the previous water tortures. The procedure itself, where a liquid is forced down the throat and into the stomach of the victim, is repeated again and again until great suffering is induced, or death occurs. It was used as a legal torture and execution method of the courts of France in the 17th and 18th century, and by the Americans against the Filipinos in the Philippine/American War of 1899-1902. The Japanese in World War II also used it in their fight against the Americans and Chinese. The Human Rights Watch organization, reports that as recently as the start of the new millennium, security forces in Uganda sometimes forced a detainee to lie face up under an open water spigot.

There is perhaps no better description of this terrible torture than the one supplied by William Lithgow, a Scotsman, who in 1620, was arrested in Malaga as a spy and thrown into the dungeons of the

Inquisition. To make him confess to something he was not, Lithgow was tortured to the limits of any human being's endurance, and it is a wonder that he ever lived to tell the tale. After suffering agonizing torture on the rack, Lithgow was subjected to forced ingestion; he says of this torture:

"He (the torturer) went to an earthen jar standing full of water, a little beneath my head: from whence carrying a pot full of water, in the bottom whereof there was an incised hole, which being stopped by his thumb, till it came to my mouth, he did pour it in my belly; the measure being a Spanish *sombre* which is an English pottle (4 pints); the first and second devices I gladly received, such was the scorching drought of my tormenting pain, and likewise I had drunk none for three days before. But afterwards, at the third charge perceiving these measures of water to be inflicted upon me as tortures, O strangling tortures! I closed my lips again-standing that eager crudelity. Whereat the Alciade enraged set my teeth asunder with a pair of iron cadges, detaining them there, at every several turn, both mainly and manually; whereupon my hunger-clunged belly waxing great, grew drum-like I bolstered, for it being a suffocating pain, in regard of my head hanging downward, and the water reingorging itself, in my throat, with a struggling force, it strangled and swallowed up my breath from yowling and groaning.

"And now to prevent my renewing grief (for presently my heart faileth and forsaketh me) I will only briefly avouch, that between each one of these seven circular charges, I was aye re-examined, each examination continuing half an hour, each half-hour a hell of internal pain, and between each torment, a long distance of life-quelling time."

PLATE 34.

Disembowelment

Som their bowells puld out And put in a basin

Disembowelment

The illustration overleaf (see PLATE 34), refers to an incident that occurred to one of the faithful during the Persecution of the Waldenses; Clarke writes:

"At *Turin* one of them had his bowels torn out of his belly, and put in a basin before his face, and then he was cruelly martyred."

Disembowelment as a torture is fatal in all cases, when performed on a living creature. Historically, used as a severe form of capital punishment, the last organs to be removed during the process would be the heart and lungs. This enabled the torturers to keep the victim alive, and therefore in pain, for as long as possible.

As mentioned earlier, disembowelment was one of the sevenfold aspects of the terrible sentence to be "hanged, drawn and quartered." Typically given to those who were convicted of high treason, the following example demonstrates how traumatic this stage of the proceedings could be. It concerns Sir Everard Digby, one of the conspirators in the infamous Gunpowder Plot of 1605:

"Digby died first - and very bravely under the most hideous circumstances. He declined to pray with Protestant pastors but asked for the prayers of all Catholics. He was calm and cheerful, saying farewell to his friends as he mounted the ladder.

"His executioner was merciless. Cut down too swiftly from his half-hanging, Digby was conscious and alert during his public castration and disembowelling. It is impossible, however, to believe Antony à Wood (citing Bacon as authority) who says that when his heart was torn out and held up with the cry, "Here is the heart of a traitor," Sir Everard answered: "Thou liest". A not dissimilar story is told of Harrison, the regicide of Charles I."[1].

In the above example it was the Protestants that tortured the Catholics; we now turn to the Ireland of 1642, where Irish Papists wreaked their vengeance on the English Protestants. There seems no horror, that fiendish human ingenuity can conceive, that has not been used at some time in the name of religion. In Kilkenny, the Papists, after beating to death an English woman, took her five-year old daughter and ripped her up abdominally, letting her guts spill out. They forced one Protestant man to attend Holy Mass and then disembowelled him leaving him to die.

In Japan, disembowelment was a method of execution and also a ritualized form of suicide typically used by the samurai class. Those privileged enough to be allowed to commit seppuku (colloquially, hara-kiri), literally "stomach cutting," found it preferable to dying at the hands of another. Committing this type of suicide condoned any or every crime and deemed the victim free from dishonour. In later times, the act of beheading the victim by a second called a kaishaku-nin, was added to the ritual to make it more humane.

More up-to-date incidents of disembowelment are cited in 'Indictment: Count Three,' in the proceedings of the Nuremberg trial for War Crimes. It states the following in connection with the subject of disembowelment:

"In the Stalingrad region more than 40,000 persons were tortured and killed. After the Germans were expelled from Stalingrad, more than a thousand mutilated bodies of local inhabitants were found with marks of torture. One hundred and thirty-nine women had their arms painfully bent backwards and

---

1. C. G. L. Du Cann *English Treason Trials* 1964 p.129.

held by wires. From some their breasts had been cut off, and their ears, fingers and toes had been amputated. The bodies bore the marks of burns. On the bodies of the men the five-pointed star was burned with an iron, or cut with a knife. Some were disembowelled."

"In the Ganov camp 200,000 peaceful citizens were exterminated. The most refined methods of cruelty were employed in this extermination, such as disembowelling and the freezing of human beings in tubs of water. Mass shootings took place to the accompaniment of the music of an orchestra recruited from the persons interned."

PLATE 35.

The Disembowelment of Pregnant Women

Womens bellyes Ript up And their Chilldren trod underfeet

The Disembowelment of Pregnant Women

The illustration (see PLATE 35) shows the sickening spectacle of women being disemboweled by their persecutors and their live children being mercilessly pulled from their wombs and trodden underfoot. It directly refers to the Persecution of the Waldenses by the President of Opede, who (see page 95), declared war on Aix and Marseilles sometime in 1540's. The incident that Clarke relates was when Opede was attacking the town of Cabrieres:

"*Opede* entering the Town, caused all the men to be brought into a field, and to be cut to pieces, the soldiers striving who should shew the best manhood in cutting off heads, arms and legs: The women he caused to be locked in a barn with much straw, and so put fire to it, where many women great with childe were burnt: One soldier moved with pity, opening a hole in the wall, that some of them might come out; *Opede* made them to be beaten back into the fire with Pikes and Halberts. Some of them that came forth he slew with his own hands, ripping open their bellies, so that their children came forth, whom he trod under his feet."

It must be remembered by the reader (see Introduction), that some of Clarke's stories, although probably truthful in their basic facts, may have a fanciful element attached to them and therefore should be read in that spirit. Here is another incident of the disembowelment of a pregnant woman that he reports occurred during the Massacre at Paris in 1572.

"A jeweller being in bed with his wife, who at that time had the midwife with her; being neer the time of her delivery, these bloody villains came knocking at the door, and in the Kings name demanded entrance; the woman as ill as she was, opened the door, whereupon rushing in, they stabbed her husband in his bed; the Midwife seeing that they were bent to murder the woman also, earnestly intreated them to tarry at least so long till the infant (which would be the twentieth child that God had given her) was born; but not withstanding her request, they took the woman, and thrust a dagger into her fundiment up to the hilt; the woman finding herself mortally wounded yet desirous to bring forth her fruit, fled into a corn-loft, whether these tigers pursuing her gave her another stab into the belly, and so cast her out of the window into the street, and upon the fall, the child came forth of her body, the head foremost, gaping and yauning in a pitiful manner.

One of these murderers snatching up a little child in his armes, the poor babe began to play with his beard, and to smile upon him; but instead of being moved to compassion, this villain, whose heart was harder then the rocks, wounded it with his dagger, and cast it all gore blood into the river."

When, as already mentioned (see page 110), the Irish Papists wreaked their terrible vengeance upon the English Protestants in Ireland in 1642; the horrendous act of disembowelling pregnant women was perpetrated by the Papists in the town of Kilkenny. Women who were far advanced in pregnancy were hung up and their bellies ripped open. The living babies were then removed and thrown to wild dogs.

Perhaps still more disturbing, is the fact that this atrocity is reported to have occurred as recently as the beginning of the new millennium. During the Sierra Leone Civil War (1991 - 2002), horrific tortures are reported to have been used upon the civilian population. The Sierra Leone's Truth and Reconciliation Commission (TRC), which was later created out of the peace process, was mandated to establish an impartial record of the abuses that occurred during the war as a step to achieving national reconciliation.

Part of this report concentrated upon the human rights violations carried out against women and young girls. It found that all armed groups carried out human rights violations against the women and girls of Sierra Leone. These included, among many other violations, killing, rape, sexual violence, amputation, and the disembowelment of pregnant women.

PLATE 36.

Removal Of Heart

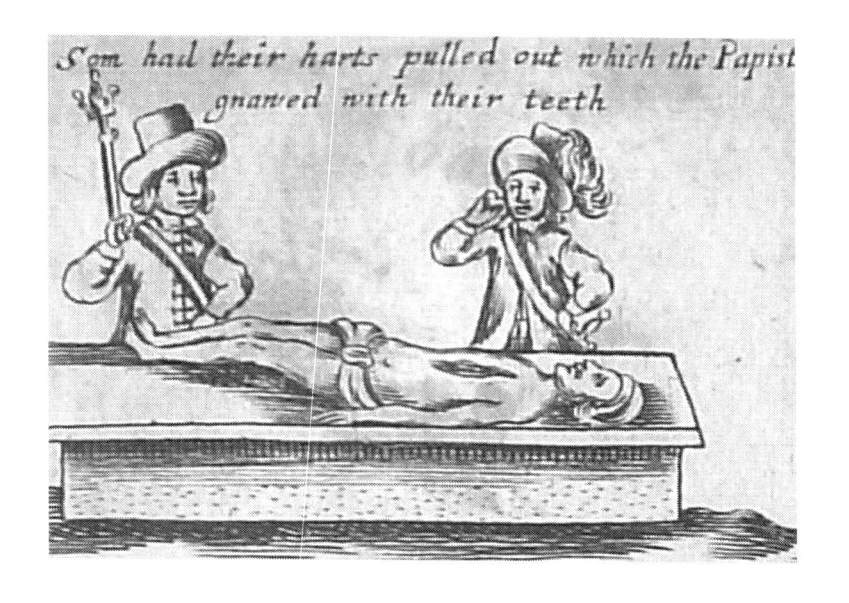

Som had their harts pulled out which the Papist gnawed with their teeth

Removal Of Heart

The heart was not only removed during the process of disembowelment; it was also taken directly by slicing through the chest. This act is pictured in the illustration (see PLATE 36.), and depicts Papists removing the heart of their victim and then gnawing on it during the persecutions that took place in France, in the early 1560's. Clarke writes of this incident:

"At *Bar* the Popish enemies entering the town, committed such cruelties as never were seen, especially against women and little children; Some of their breasts they cut open, pulled out their hearts and gnawed them with their teeth, rejoycing that they had tasted of an *Huguenots* heart."

Perhaps the most well known practitioners of this type of torture are the Aztecs, who invariably sacrificed any prisoners they took to the god Tezcatepoca. Under threat of capture, most of their enemies preferred to take their own lives than to suffer the torments that the Aztecs had in store for them. And who can blame them? Here is what the unfortunate ones could expect to happen to them.

They would be laid on their backs upon a sacrificial stone. Their arms and legs would be held firmly by the Aztec priests while a scarlet-robed executioner, holding a sharp-edged instrument, would slit open their breasts, place his hand through their wound, and rip out their warm, pulsating, heart. If they were really unlucky, they would have had their arms and legs methodically cut off, before the chest incision was made and their heart pulled out.

Reminiscent of the ancient Aztec sacrifices, are atrocities committed at a more recent date and reported in 'The Times,' for March 10, 1928. Its news item concerned the Chinese Communist atrocities that are alleged to have occurred at that time. The Reds, being driven out of Canton city, continued to pursue their terrorist activities in South-West China. Reports from various towns and villages in the area concerned gruesome forms of execution that eventually filtered through to the press. One such report, said that the terrorists had torn out the hearts of villagers and then cooked and eaten them.

A most bizarre incident relating to this particular method of torture happened while I was in the process of writing this book and concerns the murder of Taylor Powell, by his martial arts training partner, Jarrod Wyatt. According to a report contained on NYDailyNews.com. for Monday May 31, 2010:

"A California judge upheld charges of murder against a mixed martial arts fighter on Friday after the man allegedly cut the victims heart out of his chest."

Apparently, Wyatt and his 21 year-old training partner, Taylor Powell, had ingested hallucinogenic mushrooms which had caused two very different reactions in the men. Wyatt stated that while he was under the influence of the drugs, he became convinced that Powell was possessed by the devil and that it was his duty to expel the demon from him. He claims that in his drugged state he was impressed to follow a prescribed ritual; he first beat up Powell, cut out his tongue with a knife, and then used the knife to slit open Powell's chest and rip out the young man's heart. Wyatt then removed other organs from Powell's body and tossed them onto the fire because he feared that Powell was still alive and still a vessel of the devil. He said he had to be sure that Powell was dead.

The autopsy came to the conclusion that Powell was still very much alive when his heart was removed from him and very likely conscious of the fact. Wyatt therefore, together with the act of cutting out Powell's tongue, faces charges of torture as well as murder.

PLATE 37.

The Rack

The Rack

The illustration (see PLATE 37.), depicts one of the persecutions the Waldenses suffered at the hands of the Catholics in the early 1560's. Clarke writes:

"Then were they at *la Garde* cited before the Inquisitor, and many fair promises were made unto them, if they would appear; but contrary thereunto, thirty of them were apprehended, and put to the rack.

One Charlin was racked with such violence, that his bowels brake out of his belly, and all to extort from him a confession, that in the night, the candles being put out, they committed whoredome, and abominable incest, yet would he never confesse any such wickednesse."

When I first read this passage about bowels breaking out of the stomach because of being racked too violently, I thought it was perhaps an exaggeration on Clarke's behalf, especially when one looks at the type of rack used. The body *would* break under violent racking on this type of contraption, but it would be the limbs and joints of the victim's body that would suffer the breaking, not the abdomen. However, it may not be that Clarke's account is untrue; it may be just that the picture is inaccurate in its portrayal of the incident.

Several devices very similar in principal to the rack have been used through the ages. The one that seems to fit best with Clarke's description of the outcome of the racking is called the 'intestinal crank.' The procedure in this type of torture was for the torturers to make an incision in the abdomen and separate the duodenum (the first and shortest part of the small intestine) from the pylorus (the region of the stomach that connects to the duodenum). They would then attach the upper part of the stomach of the victim to a crank and rotate the crank. The rotation of the crank would extract the intestines (or bowels) from the gastrointestinal cavity of the conscious victim. I suspect that *Charlin*, may well have been a victim of this hideous contraption.

The rack, as with other instruments of torture, came in many different varieties, but its basic design (see PLATE 37.), consisted of a rectangular frame, usually made of wood, over six feet in length and supported on four legs that raised it slightly off the ground.

The victim was laid on his back, on the ground, beneath the frame, with his hands and feet secured with ropes (see illustration), to two rollers attached at either end of the frame. These two rollers turned in opposite directions, and by inserting poles into fitments on the rollers, the torturers could turn the rollers to tighten the ropes a fraction at a time, stretching the victim's body in the process. One gruesome feature about being stretched on the rack was the loud 'popping' noises the victim's cartilage, ligaments or bones made, as they snapped under the tension of the ropes. Additionally, once muscle fibres have been stretched after a certain point they lose their elasticity and are unable to contract. The victim, therefore, once released from the rack, had ineffective muscles as well as the problems arising from the breaks and dislocations he had suffered.

John Holland, the second Duke of Exeter and the constable of the Tower of London in 1447, is said to have introduced the rack to England; consequently, it became popularly known as the Duke of Exeter's daughter. Well known figures who were introduced to the charms of Exeter's daughter, were: Guy Fawkes, Edward Campion, Anne Askew and the Elizabethan dramatist Thomas Kyd.

The French, with their usual panache, decided to

improve the traditional rack by the addition of spiked rollers, which were to be inserted under the spine of the victim to cause even more pain and damage.

PLATE 38.

Children Butchered

Children Butchered

There cannot be anything more despicable than the torturing of innocent children. This, according to Clark, is precisely what the tyrant Valerianus did to appease his gods. "Valerianus", he writes; "sacrificed young infants to his Idols, quartered their bodies, divided the intrails of young children new born."

Clarke also describes the atrocities suffered by Christian children in Africa at the hands of an invading army of Vandals (see PLATE 38.).

"Guiltlesse infants felt their barbarous rage, whom they dashed against the ground, violently pulling little ones from their mothers breasts to brain them; of others, by wide stretching of their tender legs, they tore them in pieces, from the fundament."

One of the most notorious child torturers of all time was Gilles de Rais; black magician, sadist and murderer, this cold-blooded torturer of children was arrested, tried and hanged in October, 1440.

A Marshal of France, de Rais was an extensive landowner who ordered his servants to kidnap children of all ages, and both sexes, for him to sadistically torture and sacrifice to the devil. Fond of torturing innocent children, de Rais was not so keen when it came to being tortured himself. Just the mere *threat* of torture was enough to get the Marshal to admit that he had murdered 140 children - although it is alleged that in his bloody career, this unfeeling monster, had killed many more.

During the persecutions suffered by the Waldenses, around the middle of the seventeenth century, children were cut to pieces, decapitated and killed in various ways in front of their parents, but what I find more disturbing is the fact that the butchery of innocent children still continues today. As recent as

March, 1979, the 'Lakeland Ledger,' a newspaper covering the Vietnam-China border war, reported that the Vietnamese Foreign Ministry claimed:

"Chinese troops beheaded and disembowelled almost 100 children, burned and looted properties, raped women and mercilessly killed people with brutality everywhere they went."

Still more recently; News.Scotsman.com, 27 January 2008, carries the headline - "Children butchered as Kenya erupts." During clashes between rival ethnic gangs in Nakuru in Kenya's Rift Valley the article says that:

"Bodies piled up in Nakuru mortuary yesterday. The dead, including children, were scarred by machete blows, spear thrusts and arrow shots."

Only *this year*, The Sunday Times for March 8, 2010, headlined, "500 butchered in Nigerian killing fields." The article went on to say:

"Dozens of bodies lined the dusty streets of three Christian villages in Northern Nigeria yesterday. Other victims of Sunday morning's Muslim rampage were jammed into a local morgue, the limbs of slaughtered children tangled in a grotesque mess.

On toddler appeared fixed in the protective but hopeless embrace of an older child, possibly his brother. Another had been scalped. Most had severed hands and feet."

One of the most heartrending stories that I have come across (and one which I shall quote from quite extensively), was published on the MailOnline for 25 September 2009. It was written by Andrew Malone and concerns the persecution of albino children in Tanzania:

"Like a hunted animal run to ground, the little girl was cornered.

Branded a 'ghost' on account of her striking white

skin, Mariam Emmanual had been chased through her African village, in a remote corner of Tanzania, by a blood thirsty mob.

Exhausted and terrified, the five-year-old slumped in the dust at the end of an alley. She whimpered and cowered while the adults surrounded her and sharpened their knives and machetes.

Then they set to work, butchering and dividing up her remains between themselves.

'Mariam did not have the benefit of being unconscious before she died.' said one shocked investigator.

'She was killed, like an animal, by grown men who showed no compassion for another human being.'

Mariam's crime? She was an albino, one of more than 17,000 black Africans who suffer from a rare genetic condition that makes their skin white and their hair red or blond.

And in a continent where millions believe in black magic or 'muti,' their organs and blood are worth far more than their lives.

For decades, the albinos of Africa - known as the 'tribe of ghosts,' 'zeros' or the 'invisibles' - have suffered appalling treatment at the hands of their own neighbours and are murdered for their body parts, which are believed to bring good fortune and cure all manner of ills ..

In fact, the eyes, blood and organs of albinos can now fetch thousands of pounds - unimaginable sums in East Africa, where millions live on less than £2 a day and where this shocking trade is most common.

Indeed the colossal sums involved have spawned a new breed of freelance killers, often protected by the police, who harvest albino body parts for massive profits.

Some governments are trying to stamp out this vile business.

This week, the courts in Tanzania, where there have been 90 such killings in the past two years, handed out the death sentences to a group of men who had slaughtered and dismembered an albino boy - the first such punishment for albino killers.

The court in the north-west Shinyanga District, near Lake Victoria, ordered three men to hang for their part in the slaughter of Matatizo Dunia, a 14-year-old albino.

He had been bundled out of his home in the dead of night - and cut to pieces.

One of the accused was caught with the boy's leg. The remainder of the corpse was found hidden in the bushes. The guilty men admitted they planned to sell the 'white-meat' to witch doctors.

The gang is believed to have been responsible for 'hunting' albinos throughout the region, before trading their organs across this vast continent. And many are relieved that they now face the gallows."

PLATE 39.

Displaying Dismembered Body Parts

80 slaine And their q[uar]ters
set on stakes for 30
miles together

Displaying Dismembered Body Parts

During the persecution of the religious sect known as the Waldenses, Catholics dismembered the limbs of their victims (see PLATE 39.), and displayed them upon wooden stakes. Clarke writes:

"The Inquisitor *Panza* cut the throats of eighty, as butchers do sheep's; then causing them to be divided into four quarters, he set up stakes for a space of thirty miles, and appointed a quarter to be fastened to every stake."

Of course, there are many more examples of this deplorable act of dismembering and displaying of human body parts. With the introduction of the sentence to be 'Hanged, Drawn and Quartered,' into the British judiciary system, the English masses were provided with a new form of entertainment; the privilege of being able to go and see human body parts displayed all over the country. After the half-strangling, evisceration and dismembering of the victim subjected to this cruel punishment, the body parts would be shipped to the desired venue for public display (admittedly the displays were meant as a deterrent, but history tends to prove their ineffectiveness). Before display, the heads were usually boiled in seawater with cumin seeds to repel the attentions of scavenging birds, but this was not always the case, as the following example shows.

William Wallace (1272 - 1305), the inspiration for the 1995 film 'Braveheart,' was a Scottish knight and landowner who was a leading figure in the Wars of Scottish Independence at the time of Edward I.

Wallace managed to evade capture by the English until 5 August 1305, when he was handed over to English soldiers at Robroyston near Glasgow, by John de Menteith, a Scottish knight loyal to Edward. He was transported to Westminster Hall, London, where he was tried for treason.

The fact that he claimed he could not be tried for treason because he was not Edward's subject but that the absent John Balliol was his true king, didn't seem to wash with the court. He was declared guilty of treason and condemned to be Hanged, Drawn and Quartered.

On the 23 August, 1305, Wallace was taken from the hall, stripped naked, and dragged at the heels of a horse to the Elms at Smithfield. Hung until half strangled, then released from the noose and disembowelled; his bowels were burnt before his eyes. He was then beheaded and his body cut into four quarters. His head was dipped in tar to preserve it, stuck on top of a pike, and placed on London Bridge for all to see. Wallace's head was not to be alone for long; the heads of two of his compatriots, brothers John and Simon Fraser, also tried for treason were sent to join it. To underline the fact that Wallace was truly dead, his four limbs were displayed separately, in Aberdeen, Berwick-upon-Tweed, Stirling and Newcastle-upon-Tyne.

The custom of taking body parts as trophies or displaying them as a deterrent or even as objects of curiosity has been pretty well universal throughout the centuries, including our own. The Seattle Times, 20 August, 2006, reported that for $24.50 a head (no pun intended), Seattle residents would have the chance to see a collection of 21 human cadavers, Chinese in origin, along with 250 organs and partial body specimens, in an exhibition held by 'Bodies The Exhibition'.

However, critics of the exhibition, which had already appeared in six venues including London and New York, questioned the source of the bodies and the ethics in displaying human beings without consent.

Practitioners of Falun Gong (who readers are already familiar with), had picketed the 'Bodies' exhibition ever since it first opened, concerned with the provenance of the cadavers, as many of their practitioners had conveniently disappeared (convenient for the Chinese government that is).

'Bodies The Exhibition,' first opened in Tampa, Florida, on 20 August, 2005. The show, operated by Premier Exhibitions, can still be seen now in many cities around the world. Questions regarding the origin of the bodies were quite rightly asked. When New York Attorney General Andrew Chrome concluded his investigation of Premier on 29 May, 2008, he reported that:

"The grim reality is that Premier Exhibitions has profited from displaying the remains of individuals who may have been tortured and executed in China. Despite repeated denials, we now know that Premier itself cannot demonstrate the circumstances that led to the death of the individuals. Nor is Premier able to establish that these people consented to their remains being used in this manner. Respect for the dead and respect for the public requires that Premier do more than simply assure us that there is no reason for concern. This settlement is a start."

The settlement agreed with Premier was that the exhibition ended the practice of using human remains of suspect origin. This, of course, still begs the question; where *did* the withdrawn human remains come from in the first place?

PLATE 40.

Torture Of The Boots

Som had booter of boiling oile put on their legs ouer a small fire

Torture Of The Boots

During the Persecution of the Waldenses in Provence, the torture of the boots (see PLATE 40.), was carried out by a monk called John de Rosa. Clarke writes of the procedure that this torturous monk adopted:

"In the beginning of this Persecution, there was one *John de Rosa*, a Monk who gat a Commission to those he suspected to be hereticks; whereupon he afflicted the faithful with all kindes of cruelty: Amongst other horrible torments that he used, this was one; he filled boots with boiling grease, and put them upon their legs, tying them backwards over a form, and their legs hanging down over a soft fire: Thus he tormented very many, and in the end most cruelly put them to death."

The torture of the boots came in many variations; the example above is just one of them. Primitive forerunners of the archetypal torture can be found dating back centuries, but basically they tend to fall into two distinct categories regardless of the material that the boots are constructed from: Processes that use liquids to consume the flesh of the legs and feet, and those that use solid structures to break the flesh and bone. Whatever the case, the victim, if not executed, usually remained a cripple for the rest of their life. Some boots were made of iron or copper and designed to encase the naked limb from the foot to the knee, while others were made of rawhide or spongy, porous leather. One method of torture used with iron boots, was to drive wedges of wood or metal down between the apparatus and the victim's legs, thus causing serious flesh wounds, and crushing and splintering the bone of their legs. Another method using iron or copper boots (sometimes fixed in place on the floor), would be to slowly fill the boots with boiling water, oil, or even molten lead, to consume the flesh of the feet and legs.

The notorious "Spanish Boots" were iron casing boots that had a screw attachment which when turned, would painfully compress the calves of the victim's legs. The boots were sometimes heated until red-hot either before being clamped onto the legs or while being tightened up. During the process of the iron boots getting hotter, questions were put to the prisoners who were in so much pain and agony that they were likely to confess to anything.

Torture of the boots was a popular method of persuasion in Scotland where it gained such whimsical names as bootikins, buskins, cashilaws or caspicaws (warm hose). The Scottish prototype, was a vaguely boot-shaped rawhide garment that was drawn over the feet and legs of the victims, bound in place with cords and soaked with water. When the prisoner's legs were slowly heated by a fire, the rawhide would drastically contract (like the process involved in the bulls-hide torture see page 32), squeezing the limbs until the bones in the feet and legs were dislocated.

Yet another form of boot torture used in Scotland during the seventeenth century and known as Brodequins, was also used extensively in the British Isles and France. The prisoner was seated on a strong bench and a trio of upright wooden boards were placed on the outside and inside of the victim's legs and secured with strong cord. Wooden or metal wedges were then hammered between the centre board and the prisoner's legs, causing the cords to bite painfully through the victim's flesh as well as the boards dislocating and crushing the bones.

As I started this section with Catholics using the torture of the boots, I will finish with an example of the Protestants using the same. In 1570, Queen Elizabeth I, was excommunicated from the Catholic church, in the Papal Bull, 'Regnans in Excelsis.' Afterwards, feelings against Catholics were running high both in Britain and in Ireland which inevitably led to the revolt by Irish Catholics known as the Second Desmond Rebellion (1579 - 1583).

It was during the height of this rebellion, in 1581, that Pope Gregory XIII appointed Dermot O'Hurley (c 1530 - 1584), as the Roman Catholic Archbishop of Cashel. After his consecration, O'Hurley arranged to be smuggled back into Ireland where he arrived at Holmpatrick Stand in County Dublin in 1583, as the rebellion was drawing to a close.

O'Hurley stayed with Baron Thomas Flemyng at Slane while he spread Catholicism throughout the territories of the of the O'reilly clan. Unfortunately the archbishop's letters, which had arrived by another ship, had been intercepted by the priest hunters and Flemyng, under pain of severe penalties, was forced to hand over O'Hurley to the authorities. On the 8 October 1583, the archbishop was imprisoned in Dublin Castle.

One of the severe tortures that Dermot O'Hurley underwent to force him to embrace Protestantism consisted of lightweight metal boots into which both his feet and legs were placed. The boots were then filled with cold water and the archbishop's feet and legs heated over a fire until the water boiled aggressively.

Despite these severe tortures, O'Hurley stood his ground (again no pun intended), and according to surviving correspondence between Dublin and Whitehall, the Queen, who wanted the archbishop to have a fair trial under English Law, finally gave into Sir Francis Walsingham, and approved a trial by military tribunal. O'Hurley was tried for treason and sentenced to death.

Still proclaiming his innocence, the archbishop was hanged outside the walls of Dublin, on the

morning of Saturday, 20 June, 1584.

PLATE 41.

Forced To Carry Weight

Forced To Carry Weight

The illustration (see PLATE 41.), refers to a torture used in the persecution of the church in Africa in 427 A.D. Clarke writes of this torture:

"Many of the Ministers and Nobles they loaded with mighty burthens, as if they had been Camels or Horses, and made them carry them after them, and if they went slowly, they hasted them with iron pricks and goads, so that some of them under their burthens gave up the ghost."

A more recent example of this type of torture, i.e. a person being forced to carry weight against their will, is claimed to have occurred in England during the Second World War, and it is *still*, in fact, practised in many parts of the world, even as I write. The alleged torture that took in England during the Second World War was uncovered by the Guardian Newspaper and reported in an article dated 12 November, 2005.

The article concerns three mansion houses (nos. 6, 7, and 8), located in Kensington Palace Gardens, London. Between July 1940 and September 1948, these three mansion houses were run by MI 19, the section of the War Office responsible for interrogating prisoners of war. The establishment itself, the London office of the Combined Services Detailed Interrogation Centre, became known colloquially as the London Cage.

By examining thousands of documents relating to the establishment; some from the National Archives (formerly the Public Record Office), and others from the International Committee of the Red Cross in Geneva, The Guardian Newspaper claims to have established what happened to the prisoners incarcerated there. They write:

"The London Cage was used partly as a torture

centre, inside which large numbers of German officers and soldiers were subjected to systematic ill-treatment. In total, 3,573 men passed through the Cage, and more than 1,000 were persuaded to give statements about war crimes. The brutality did not end with the war; moreover, a number of German civilians joined the servicemen who were interrogated there up to 1948."

Within the National Archives, the Guardian found a long and detailed letter of complaint from S.S. captain, Fritz Knoechein, who describes his treatment after being taken to the Cage in October, 1946. Included in a long list of alleged tortures, he says, he and another prisoner were taken in the gardens behind the mansions, where they were forced to run in circles while carrying heavy logs.

More recently, the Amnesty International Home Library for 13 December, 2000, quotes an example of the torture under discussion, in an article entitled, 'Myanmar - The Institution of Torture.'

Human right violations in the Union of Myanmar (Burma), are of a long standing concern not only for human right organizations, but for the international community as a whole. The military regime in control of Myanmar is one of the most repressive and abusive in operation today. Torture in Myanmar has become institutionalized and is inflicted by the army not only upon insurgents but also on civilians. Amnesty International says that:

"Ethnic minority civilians living in areas of counter-insurgency operations by the Myanmar army, or *tatmadaw*, are also at risk of torture and ill-treatment. Members of ethnic minorities in areas where armed opposition groups are active have been seized by the *tatmadaw* and interrogated and tortured to extract information about the whereabouts of armed ethnic minority groups. In addition they face torture and ill-treatment when they are taken by the *tatmadaw* and forced to carry heavy supplies as porters for days or weeks at a time. If they are not able to keep up with the military column, they are severely beaten and kicked by troops. Ethnic minority women in areas of counter-insurgency activities can also be at risk of rape if they are taken to porter for the military."

Turning to China; the report of the Falun Gong Human Rights Working Group, Issue 03, talks about torture methods created by the authorities of Shifu Town. It says that since July 1999, Falun Gong practitioners have been arrested and detained by the local authorities of Shifu Town, Changyi City, Shandong Province. In order to force the practitioners to renounce Falun Gong they have used various tortures; although an unusual variant, it is no.4 on the list of tortures that we are interested in:

"4. Forcing to carry heavy items on the head.

Falun Gong practitioners were forced to carry heavy items on their heads. Wei Tiankui and Gong Zhiqiang forced practitioners Ms. Wang Lizhen to walk down stairs in a squatting position with heavy rocks weighing more than 34 lbs. loaded on top of her head. Ms. Li Xiufen was forced to walk around in a half-squatting position loaded with logs on her head. Mr. Yu Shenghe was forced to stand on gravel with five to six bricks on his head. Once Wei Tiankui placed a coal block weighing about 45 lbs. on Mr. Yu's head. Wei also placed a basin of water on Mr. Yu's head and then whipped him with an electrical cord."

Perhaps more disturbing, is the fact that the use of this particular type of torture appears to be sanctioned by the United States of America's armed forces. On the 1st of July, 2009, Ahmed al-Darbi, a Saudi national, made a written declaration concerning his detention at Bagram Air Force Base in Afghanistan, and his nearly six year imprisonment at the U.S. Navel Station at Guantánamo Bay, Cuba.

In June, 2002, Ahmed al-Darbi, was arrested at Baku airport by the Azerbaijani authorities, and in August, 2002, handed over to U.S. agents. He was then held prisoner at Bagram for about eight months before being transferred to Guantánamo Bay towards the end of March, 2003.

It was while Ahmed al-Darbi, detainee number 264, was being held at Bagram, that he claims the torture took place:

"44. I was also forced to carry boxes filled with water bottles while my hands were cuffed together. I could carry two boxes but the guards often tried to make me carry as many as four, and would hit me when I struggled. This labour caused me sciatic pain and back pain for several years."

PLATE 42.

Twisted Cords Torture and Execution

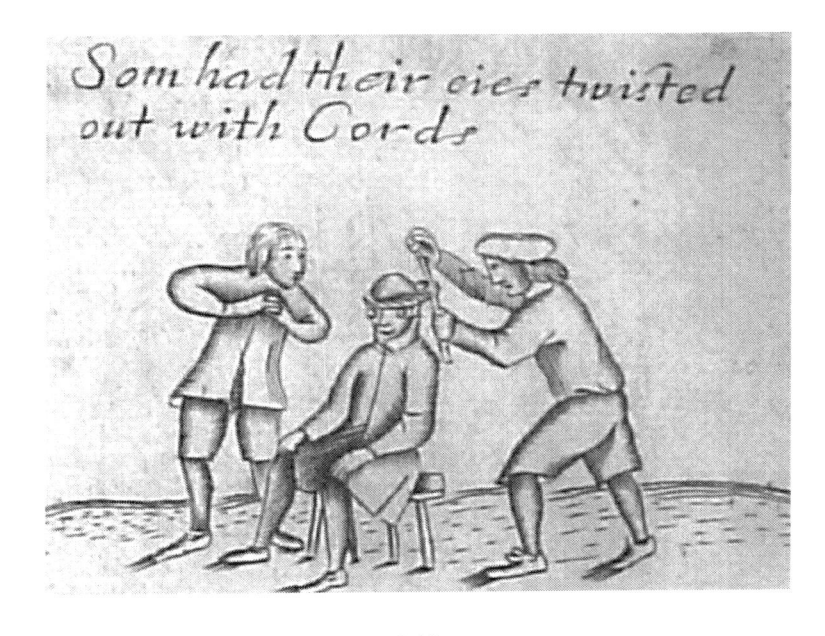

Som had their eies twisted out with Cords

Twisted Cords Torture and Execution

During the persecution of the church in Germany, which began in the year 1630, many tortures were inflicted upon Christians to extort their valuables. The use of twisted cords (cordeles), as a torture, was just one of the means used (see PLATE 42.). Samuel Clarke writes of this torture:

"If they suspected that any had hidden their gold or silver, they used exquisite torments to make them confess it; they wound and tied about the heads of some strong matches or cords, and with short truncheons twist them till blood came out of their eyes, ears, and noses, yea sometimes till their eyes started out of their heads."

Pirates of old were not renowned for their patience, and they certainly did not lack ingenuity when it came to getting information as to the whereabouts of any valuables on board their captured ships. All of passengers and crew of the ill-fated vessel were only too aware of the hideous tortures that they were likely to undergo if they did not talk.

One of the fastest and most effective tortures in the pirates' arsenal was called 'woolding', taken from the word used to describe the binding of cords around a mast. All that was required was for a short length of rope or cord to be placed around the victim's head and the ends of the rope to be secured onto a piece of wood to act as a lever. The pirate would then twist the piece of wood in a circular motion thus tightening the cords against the victim's temples, which would eventually force the eyes of the victim from their sockets. Woolding, is of course, just another name for the cordeles torture, described above.

The head not the only area of the body to be subjected to cordeles; sometimes the agonies of the rack were varied with this mode of torture and then it would be the arms and the legs of the victim that would suffer. Cords would be wound around each limb of the prisoner and passed through holes in the sides of the rack and attached to sticks. When the levers were twisted, the cords would tighten, causing terrible wounds as they cut the victim's flesh to the bone.

Not only were women not exempt from this cruel torture, *pregnant* women could also be tortured in this way:

"Pregnancy has always been deemed a sufficient reason for at least postponing the infliction, but the Madrid tribunal, in instructions of 1690, only make the concession of placing a pregnant woman on a seat, in place of binding them on the rack, while applying the exceedingly severe torture of the garrote -- sharp cord, two on each arm and two on each leg, bound around the limb and twisted with a short lever."[1].

You will notice that the author of the above passage has used the term 'garrote' when describing the process that the pregnant woman was subjected to. The term garrote (garotte, garrotte), is a Spanish word normally used when cordeles is applied to the neck of the victim for the purposes of execution.

Originally, garrottes as a means of execution, were nothing more than an upright wooden posts with a holes bored through them. The prisoner to be executed would stand or sit in front of the post, and a rope would be placed around his or her neck and the ends passed through the hole. The executioner would then pull or twist the ends of the cord until

---

1. Henry Charles Lea *A History of the Inquisition of Spain* Volume 3, Available on THE LIBRARY OF IBERIAN RECOURCES ONLINE.

the victim was dead. A later modification to this crude apparatus was the introduction of a spike, fixed to the post behind the prisoner's neck, in order to separate the vertebrae as the victim was slowly strangled.

The apparatus that was used in China was different to the one that I have described but the process rendered the same result - *slow* strangulation. The Illustrated London News for Saturday, 4 April, 1857, carries three illustrated scenes, with appended narrative, of garrotting Chinese style.

The first scene shows the prisoner, with hands bound behind his back, being led to his place of execution by a length of chain fastened around his neck. A flat lath of wood, which is also, "attached to his neck in such a manner as to project above his head, bears in Chinese characters, a description of his crime."

When the victim arrives at the site of his execution, the chain and the wooden lath attached to his neck are removed and he is secured to a thin beamed, wooden crucifix (possibly bamboo poles), the horizontal beam of which, is level with the outstretched arms of the prisoner as he stands upright. Fixed to the horizontal beam, just behind the prisoner's neck, is a small, square, wooden frame, to support the lever while it is under tension and being operated by the executioner. A cord is placed around the victim's neck and both ends are passed through the small, square, framework, and attached to a longer stick which acts as the lever.

The second scene of the series shows the executioner slowly tightening the cords "by means of the lever till blood gushes from the eyes, nose, ears, and mouth of the culprit."

Whatever the crime of the prisoner (which may have been quite minor in comparison to the severity of the sentence), his ordeal, and indeed his family's ordeal, is not yet over; his head is removed from his body and placed in a small cage, attached to a long pole. The pole, along with the head, is carried back to the victim's home and erected outside his door.

"The last scene shows the head of the criminal exposed in a cage whilst, as a climax to the punishments, his children are by the merciful consideration of the Celestial authorities, made to take a moral lesson by looking at the disfigured head of their dead father."

PLATE 43.

The Burning of Multiple Victims

148

The Burning of Multiple Victims

Samuel Clarke's illustration (see PLATE 43.), depicts the burning of a ship containing eighty Christian Ministers. Clarke writes that this incident occurred during the persecution of the church by the Arians that began in 339 A.D:

"In *Constantinople* the *Arrians*, favoured by the Emperour, crowed insolently over the Christians, they scourged, reviled, imprisoned, merced and laid upon them all the intollerable burthens they could device. Hereupon eighty godly Ministers in the name of the rest, addressed themselves to the Emperour, complaining of the outrages that were done to them, craving some relief: But this cruel Tyrant commanded *Modestus* the Generall of his Army, to embark them all in a ship, as if he would have sent them into banishment, but secretly he gave direction to the Marriners, to set the ship on fire, and to retire themselves into a boat, and so these holy Martyrs glorified in the Name of Christ, by patient suffering of a double death, burning and drowning."

Clarke says that nearly a hundred years later, when the Arians invaded Africa, that an Arian Tyrant would once again treat Christians in the same cruel manner:

"Then did he cause a ship to be filled with combustible matter, commanded that these holy Martyrs should be put into it, and fast bound in the same, and fire to be set to the ship in the sea, that they might be burned to death."

Of course, ships were not the only places that Christians were burned in groups. If the reader recalls, in the section on the disembowelment of pregnant women that Clarke, when speaking of the

President of Opede (see p. 113), writes:

"The women he caused to be locked in a barn with much straw, and so put fire to it, where many women great with childe were burnt."

For a far more severe example of this type of atrocity one need look no further than Samuel Clarke's account of the persecutions of the Christians by the emperor Maximian (c.250 - 310, joint Roman Emperor with, although always subordinate to, Diocletianus):

"Also many Christians of all ages and sorts, being met together in a Church, to celebrate the memoriall of Christs nativity, Maximian the Emperour sent some to fire the Church, and burnt them all: But first they commanded a cryer to proclaim, that whosoever would have life, should come out and sacrifice to *Jupiter*, otherwise they should all be burnt: Then one stepping up boldly, in the name of all the rest, said, We are all Christians, and believe that Christ is our only God and King, and we will sacrifice to none but him: Hereupon the fire was kindled, and some thousands of men, woman and children were burnt in that place."

Claims of murder on such a grand scale as the above are difficult to substantiate. However, George Ryley Scott, in his book, 'The History of Torture Throughout The Ages,' writes of the emperor Diocletianus (244 - 311), the senior member of the Diocletianus/Maximian partnership:

"Diocletianus, however, surpassed all his predecessors in the extent and severity of his persecutions. By his express orders, 20,000 Christians were burnt in the Church of Nicodemia."[1].

Could this have been the same massacre that Clarke speaks of?

1. George Ryley Scott, p.143, *The History of Torture Throughout The Ages*, Seventh Impression 1959.

It was not always the Christians who suffered this cruel end. It is reported in 'The Times,' for 3 March, 1928, that the Communists, continuing their terrorist activities in South-West China, locked 300 Buddhist monks in their temple and set fire to it, killing all inside.

Unfortunately, there are still more recent examples of this atrocity taking place. 'RepublicReport.com,' who claim "to stand against the prevailing terror-based culture of Islamic-Extremists in Northern Nigeria," report that in:

"September 2001, Jos (Northern Nigeria) in a well planned and highly coordinated program Islamic-jihadists attack Christians in Jos, burning down churches, and private homes of Christians, looting the churches and private property of Christians. Hundreds of churches were burned and thousands of Christians were slaughtered some burned while worshipping in their churches."

It is debatable how accurate this report is; it is certainly true to say that since 1999, more than 10,000 Nigerians have been killed, both Muslim and Christian, in sectarian attacks and reprisals between the two religions, but I suspect that the casualty figures for the Christians in this report are somewhat exaggerated. However, it cannot be denied that the incidents spoke of took place, they are, unfortunately, *still* taking place in Nigeria as I write.

I conclude with another example of people being burnt to death in their place of worship in Nigeria, this time reported on the 'World Socialist Web Site,' for the 4 June, 2004. The 'Obsanjo' referred to in the text is Olusegun Obsanjo, President of Nigeria from 1999 - 2007. The account also refers to the 2001 troubles, but puts the death toll at "more than one thousand," not the "thousands" reported by RepublicReport.com:

"Plateau State has been beset by such ethnic

clashes in the years since Obsanjo came to power, the worst being the violence that erupted in Jos city in September 2001 and caused more than one thousand deaths. The following year, Christian Tarok farmers killed the cattle of the nomadic Muslim Fulani herders, and this led to revenge attacks on a number of Christian villages. In February 2004, Muslim youths attacked a Christian hamlet not far from Yelwa. A few days later, a church in Yelwa was set on fire, killing 49 of the people inside."

PLATE 44.

Torture by Using Animals

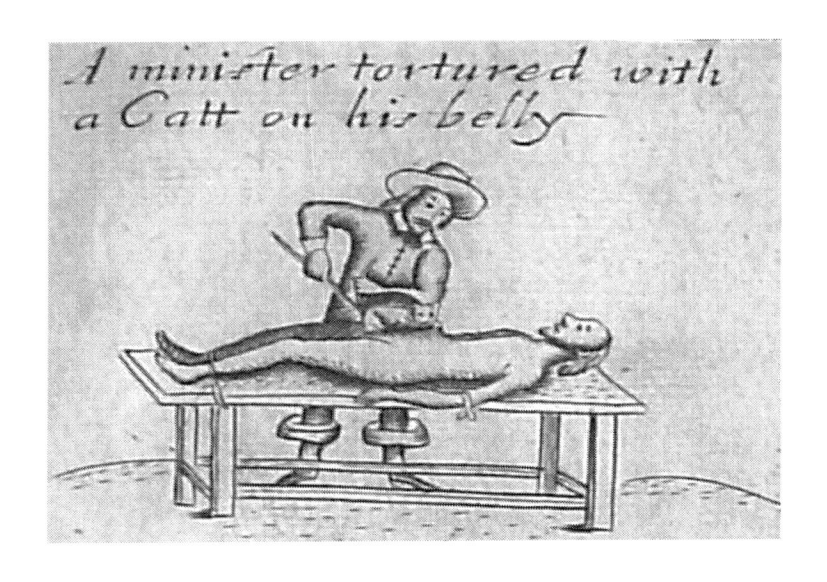

Torture by Using Animals

The torturing of human beings by the use of animals has been the custom and practice of many races throughout the centuries. The torture inflicted may be just the straightforward throwing of the victim to large wild beasts, as already discussed (see page 44), or it may take on a more subtle guise.

The torture illustrated (see PLATE 44), was referred to by Clarke in his martyrology as "A Minister killed with a cat," and used the services of an ordinary cat as an instrument of torture:

"One reverend aged Devine they stripped, bound him backwards upon a table, and let a big cat upon his naked belly, beating and pricking the cat to make her fix her teeth and claws therein. So that both man and cat, with hunger, pain and anguish breathed their last."

A cat was also used as an instrument during a threat of torture that took place in India, and which, mercifully, was not carried out.

Before the time of the English occupancy in India, the practice of torture was widespread for a very large number of offences both religious and civil. Sanctioned by the state; police, tax collectors, and other officials used torture routinely for inducing payment of dues and debts, eliciting confessions, and securing evidence in criminal cases. It was not unknown for these corrupt officials to use torture for their own illegal purposes.

During the seventeenth century, a vizier with a company of armed men paid a visit to a wealthy Hindoo family. The vizier demanded the man's money; a demand which was refused by the man who had his money well secreted somewhere in the house. Enraged, the vizier had his men use a series of tortures upon his prisoner to induce him to confess where his money was hidden. After two days and nights the victim still courageously bore the tortures inflicted without revealing his secret and the vizier fearing his prisoner might die, resorted to another course of action.

The victim had an infant son, an only child. The vizier's men brought the child, along with a sack containing a fierce cat, into the room where his father was being held. Putting the child in the sack with the cat, the men tied up the end and stood over the sack with bamboo sticks, ready to beat the bag and enrage the animal to destroy the child at the vizier's signal. The mere threat was enough for the father of the child to divulge the whereabouts of his money.

The placing of a victim in sack with animals, as a form of torture, had been used at a much earlier date than the example given above: Epiphanes ordered Ulpianus, after being scourged, to be put in an ox-hide sack along with a dog and a poisonous snake and thrown into the sea.

In medieval times the use of rats was considered to be a very cheap and effective way of torturing someone. There were many variants of this torture but the most common way was to restrain the victim face up and to place a rat on his or her naked stomach covered by a metal container. The container would be gradually heated and the rat having no other means of escape, would slowly tunnel through the prisoner's abdomen, causing the victim of this cruel torture an agonizingly painful, and an invariably slow form of death.

It is documented that Diederick Sonoy, an ally of William I, Prince of Orange (1533 - 1584), used a very similar technique on his prisoners to that of the one described above, during the Dutch Revolt. He would place a pottery bowl filled with rats, open side down

PLATE 45.

Animals In Dungeons

Som Cast into dungeons amongst frogge and toades

on the naked bodies of his victims, and then pile heated charcoal on top of the bowl. Like above, the rats being driven mad by the heat had no where else to go other than straight through the prisoners' stomachs.

In the illustration overleaf (see PLATE 45.), animals confined with the victim in a dungeon constitutes the torture. It shows Peter Mioce, a Christian convert, being, according to Clarke; "let down into a deep dungeon full of toads and other vermine." I suspect the other vermin that Clarke refers to may well have been rats.

One dungeon that was *definitely* full of rats was situated in the Tower of London and became infamously known as "Dungeon of the Rats." The floor of this dungeon was below high-water mark for the River Thames and was used to house condemned prisoners for the purpose of extracting confessions. When the tide of the river rose, the dungeon became full of stinking water and hordes of hungry rats. For the prisoners to sleep was to court injury or death. In the dark, stinking, waterlogged cell, the prisoners had to fight off the rats until they became so weary and exhausted, they could fight no longer.

It was not only the Tower of London where such wretched conditions existed: 'The State of the Prisons' published by John Howard in 1784 and detailing the conditions prevalent in English jails at the time, contained a most disturbing report. At the prison for town debtors in Knaresborough, in Yorkshire, Howard discovered a cell approximately 14 feet by 12 feet that contained an uncovered sewer that ran right through the middle of it. He writes:

"I was informed, that an officer, confined here some years since, for a few days, took in with him a dog to defend him from vermin; but the dog was soon destroyed, and the prisoner's face much disfigured by them."

PLATE 46.

Cords Through Limbs

Cords Through Limbs

According to Clarke, this torture (see PLATE 46.), was another one of those used during the 1630 persecution of the church in Germany, to extort valuables from the Christians. He says of the torture inflicted on the victims:

"With bodkins they made holes, or with knives they cut the skin and flesh of many. They drew strings and cords through the fleshie parts of some, and through the muscles of their thighs, legs, armes, &c. or through their noses, ears, lips, &c."

On 25 January, 1655, an order was issued under the sanction of the Duke of Savoy that precipitated another vicious persecution of the religious sect known as the Waldenses, who had now settled in the Piedmont valleys to escape from the previous persecutions by the Roman Catholic Church. The nature of the heresy that the Waldenses (or Vaudois), were accused of committing, and which the Catholics were once again ready to persecute them for, has long been established.

In 1173, Valdo, a rich merchant of Lyons, hearkening to Jesus's parable of the rich young man, gave away all of his possessions and became a beggar in order to obtain salvation and perfection in the eyes of the Lord. A group formed around Valdo intent on emulating his vow of poverty, and following the example of Christ's apostles, began to preach to others. The Pope of the Catholic Church, although impressed by their piety, imposed restrictions on their preaching which in all consciousness the Waldenses felt they had to disobey. In consequence, in 1181 they were excommunicated, and in 1184 they were formerly condemned as heretics.

The later persecution of the Waldenses by the

Catholics, following the edict 1655, was one of the cruelest and bloodiest ever to be reported. One eyewitness (cited in Samuel Morland, London, 1658), claims that an armed multitude fell upon the Wadenses in a furious manner with dead bodies strewing the streets intermingled with the groans and cries of the dying. In one village the Catholics, both civilian and soldiers, cruelly tortured some 150 women and children by beheading the women and dashing out the brains of the children. In Villaro and Bobio anyone over the age of fifteen years who refused to go to mass, was crucified with their heads downwards.

The Catholic soldiers, in particular, exercised their lust for cruelty against the supposed heretics. Mary Raymondet had her flesh sliced piece by piece from her bones until she died in frightful agony. Anne Charbonierre was transfixed upon a stake and left to die slowly while Bartholomew Frasche (more in line with the torture under discussion), had holes bored through his heels, ropes passed through his wounds, and was then dragged off to a dungeon where he died.

PLATE 47.

Drawing and Quartering

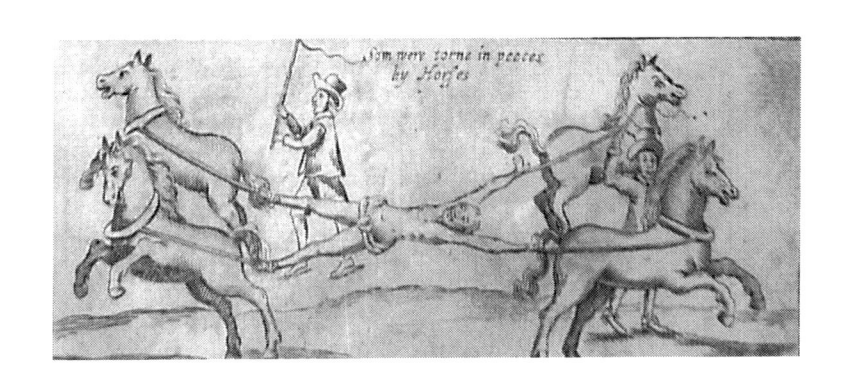

Sim were torne in peeces by Horses

Drawing and Quartering

Drawing and quartering, an ancient and long lived method of execution in European civilization, where the limbs of the victim were literally pulled apart by the use of horses (see PLATE 47.), appears to have been little known in Britain. There, the nearly as equally barbaric form of drawing and quartering as part of the hanging method of execution (see p. 57), was the order of the day.

Drawing and quartering, in its more ancient form, as revolting as it appears, was not always sufficient in itself to satisfy the demands of justice, and it was often supplemented with various other forms of torture. Prior to execution in this way, it was almost customary to lacerate the breasts, hands and thighs, of the victim, in order to pour molten lead or boiling pitch into the wounds.

On completion of these preliminary tortures, the prisoner would then have a stout rope attached to each limb and each rope-end harnessed to one of the four horses involved in the execution (see illustration). The four horses were then encouraged to give short, sharp, jerks, on the ropes, to cause the victim intolerable agony. When the executioners were happy that they had inflicted sufficient pain upon the unfortunate victim, they simultaneously whipped the four horses in different directions with the intention of ripping the victim's body to pieces.

In some instances the prisoner's body refused to be quartered no matter how much force was applied. In these cases the executioners would chop away merrily at victim's limbs with hatchets until they became separated from the still living trunk. One can well imagine that the whole torturous procedure often took quite a time to carry out.

Conclusion

The foregoing are just a sample of the tortures conceived by the dark-side of mans' nature. There are many more types of torture, both psychological and physical, that are equally as dreadful as the ones illustrated and discussed in this work. It makes one wonder whether there are *any* bounds to mans' fiendish ingenuity, when it comes to inflicting pain and suffering on his fellow man.

Printed in Great Britain
by Amazon